Welcome to the Resource Guide

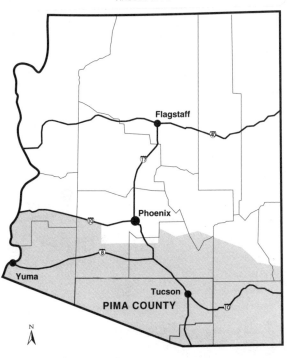

Southern Arizona's scenic landscapes offer some of the best trails-based outdoor recreation opportunities in North America. From rolling jeep roads on the saguaro cactus-studded Sonoran Desert floor to technical singletrack high in the region's "Sky Island" mountain ranges, southern Arizona enjoys natural and recreational diversity that few areas can match. Add cordial and cooperative relations between trail users and accommodating and forward-looking public land managers, and it's easy to see why many regard southern Arizona as a true *trails paradise.*

The *Southern Arizona Trails Resource Guide* was created to help trails enthusiasts of all interests and backgrounds discover southern Arizona's extensive inventory of outstanding recreational trails, and to help ensure that its trails are enjoyed safely and responsibly. The *Guide* contains a wide range of basic trails-related information, all of which will put you on the road to becoming a well-informed, well-prepared and hopefully well-satisfied southern Arizona trail user.

The *Southern Arizona Trails Resource Guide* was developed by John Dell and Steve Anderson in partnership with **Pima Trails Association** and the **Pima County Parks and Recreation Department**. Pima Trails Association is an all-volunteer, nonprofit trails advocacy group composed of equestrians, hikers, and mountain bicyclists that was founded in 1987 to protect and preserve recreational trails in Pima County. PTA's activities include trails planning, new trail development, user education, volunteer trail maintenance, and trails advocacy at the local, state, and national levels. A membership form is located on the last page of the *Guide.*

The Pima County Parks and Recreation Department was founded in 1947 and presently manages 31,000 acres of natural resource parks in Pima County that contain a wide variety of trail opportunities for hikers, mountain bicyclists, and equestrians. The agency is home to the county's trails and open space program, which is managed by a full-time trails and open space coordinator.

The principal contributor of funding for this publication is Lost Corner Tours, a Tucson-based company that specializes in educational adventures to off-the-beaten path locations, both domestic and international.

This publication was also funded in part through a grant from Recreational Equipment, Inc. (REI). REI is one of America's leading outdoors products retailers and a generous benefactor of outdoors causes.

© 1998 John D. Dell

Contents

Before You Venture Out: Important Trail Safety Information 4
    Proper Preparation for Trail Use in Southern Arizona 4
    Sharing the Trail: The Rules All Trail Users Should Know 5
    Emergency and Rescue Contacts 7
Where the Trails Are: Public Lands in Southern Arizona 8
    Public Lands Locator Map 8
    Federal Public Lands 9
        A Word About Wilderness 9
        U.S. Department of Agriculture, Forest Service 9
        U.S. Department of Interior, National Park Service 14
        U.S. Department of Interior, Bureau of Land Management (BLM) 19
        U.S. Department of Interior, Fish and Wildlife Service 25
        U.S. Department of Defense 28
        U.S. Department of Interior, Bureau of Reclamation 29
    State of Arizona 30
        Arizona State Parks 30
        Arizona State Land Department 32
        Arizona Game and Fish Department 33
    Local Government Jurisdictions 34
        Pima County Parks and Recreation Department 34
        Pima County River Park System 36
            Pima County River Park Map 36
        Trailheads in the Tucson Metro Area 37
            Trailheads Map 37
        City of Yuma 43
    Barrier-Free Facilities 44
Where the Trails Are: Other Lands in Southern Arizona 46
    Tribal Jurisdictions 46
    Nature Conservancy Preserves 46
    A Note About Private Lands 48
Trail Projects, Programs and Events 49
    The Arizona Trail 49
        Arizona Trail - Southern Arizona Route Map 49
    The Juan Bautista de Anza National Historic Trail 53
        Anza Trail Route Map 53
    The Arizona State Trails Program 54
    The Arizona Off-Highway Vehicle Program 55
    The Arizona Heritage Fund 56
    Pima County Trails and Open Space Program 56
    National Trails Day 57
Doing Your Part: Volunteering for Trails 58
    Directory of Trails Organizations 60
Trails Publications 65
Pima Trails Association Membership Form 71

Before You Venture Out: Important Trail Safety Information

Proper Preparation for Trail Use in Southern Arizona

The southern Arizona desert and its mountainous regions are beautiful, but they can also be very dangerous if you venture into them unprepared. We strongly recommend that you study the basic trip preparation advice provided below, and supplement this information with further reading on the subject. A list of helpful books can be found in the Outdoor Preparedness and First Aid section of the *Guide*'s bibliography.

- **Careful trip planning** should be the foundation of every excursion. Know where you're going, and what to expect when you get there. Study the appropriate maps and guidebooks, and take them along. Call the agencies that manage the land you'll be visiting to check on current conditions and get advice. If you'll be leading a group, thoroughly scout the trip in advance. Don't forget to check the weather report before you leave.
- **Water** is an essential element of any trails outing. Water is rarely available at trailheads, so be sure to take plenty with you—at least two quarts to a gallon for a short day trip—and replace your fluids as you go. Don't forget to provide plenty for your trail stock as well.
- **Abundant sunshine** allows us to enjoy trails year-round in southern Arizona, but the effects of the sun can be brutal. Prolonged sun exposure will damage your skin, and can cause skin cancer, the fastest growing type of cancer. Limit your time in the sun during its most intense hours (10 A.M.–3 P.M.), and cover up with long sleeves, a hat, and bandanna. Use plenty of sunscreen with a high SPF, and protect your eyes with a good pair of sunglasses.
- **Weather extremes** are the nature of the desert. The searing heat of the day can turn cold by nighttime, so be ready. Take a jacket to protect you if you're caught out overnight. Hypothermia can occur at temperatures well above freezing—in fact, as high as 50 degrees or more—so have the ability to cover up. Flash floods are a hazard in the desert; stay out of washes and canyon bottoms during thunderstorms, or if rain is occurring further up the drainage. Never attempt to drive across a running wash, even if it looks shallow—you may be risking your life. If lightning is accompanying a storm, stay off peaks and exposed ridges, and away from lone trees or rocks.
- **Essential gear** to take on any trails outing in addition to your water, maps, and jacket include:
    - Flashlight with extra batteries and bulb
    - Compass

- Food supply (an energy bar or two at a minimum)
- Extra clothing, including rain gear
- Basic first aid supplies
- Matches in a waterproof container
- Signaling mirror
- Space blanket
- Pocket knife
- Whistle
- Plastic garbage bag
- Fire starter (candle stub, heat tabs, etc.)
- Comb and a tweezer for removing cactus spines
- Well broken-in hiking boots or cycling shoes and synthetic socks, which wick moisture and help prevent blisters.

• **Venomous creatures** exist throughout southern Arizona, and their bites can be life-threatening. Avoiding an encounter, however, is usually a matter of common sense. Stay alert, and travel with care. Don't put your hands or feet in places you can't see, and if bitten, stay calm and seek immediate medical attention.

Sharing the Trail

To preserve the exceptional harmony between trail users we presently enjoy in southern Arizona, and to help protect the region's sensitive natural resources, always observe the following **Rules of the Trail**:

Guidelines for all trail users:
- Avoid solo trail use, especially in areas unfamiliar to you.
- Make sure someone knows where you're going, and when you expect to return.
- Respect private property. Obey all signs and trail markers. Secure permission before you enter or cross private property. Close gates behind you.
- Practice minimum impact trail use. Stay on existing trails. Never cut corners or switchbacks. If traveling cross-country, tread lightly to minimize resource impacts and the creation of "wildcat" or "social" trails.
- Keep your party small and together, and don't block the trail.
- In backcountry areas, leave pets at home. Otherwise, keep them leashed (it's the law).
- Downhill traffic yields to uphill traffic.
- Travel quietly. Consider the needs and feelings of others.
- Don't attempt excursions beyond your physical abilities. Get in shape first.
- When overtaking another trail user, make your presence known well in advance.
- Always yield the right-of-way to trail stock, including llamas and goats.
- Always pack out your trash, and more if possible.
- Leave flowers, rocks, and other resources in their natural state. *Never, ever*, feed or intentionally disrupt wildlife or livestock.
- Appreciate archaeological and historic sites, but don't disturb them or take souvenirs.

- Develop an environmental ethic. Volunteer to help maintain trails whenever you can.

Rules for horses and other trail stock:
- Confirm that trail stock is allowed on the trails you'd like to use *before* you ride.
- Travel at a safe pace, and be especially careful when visibility is limited.
- Wear the appropriate safety gear, including a helmet.
- Remember that trail stock can be intimidating to other users, and act accordingly.
- Trail stock can be especially hard on wet trails; avoid using them if possible.
- Don't tie trail stock directly to trees. Use a picket line (a rope stretched between two trees) instead, and place a saddle blanket or other insulator between the rope and the tree. Change the location of picket lines every day to reduce ground impact.
- Don't tie stock within 200 feet of streams, lakes or meadows.
- Clean up manure whenever possible.
- Saddle horses should yield to pack stock.
- Animals known to be skittish or unstable should *not* be used on public trails.

Rules for mountain bicyclists:
- Mountain bicyclists must yield to *all* other trail users.
- Ride only on trails you know are open to bikes. If you're unsure, inquire first.
- Federally designated wilderness areas are closed to mountain bikes.
- Always ride with care. Maintain a safe speed. Expect to find someone on the trail around every corner, and be prepared to stop quickly.
- Use extra care when approaching horses and other trail stock. Stop your bike, announce your presence by speaking calmly, and move to the downhill side of the trail. Ask the rider for special instructions, and avoid sudden movements that might startle the stock.
- Think safety. Always wear a helmet and the appropriate safety gear.
- Never intentionally disrupt livestock or wildlife.
- Ride *over* water bars, not around them.
- Carry enough tools, spares, and gear to get you home. Self-sufficiency should be your goal.

Rules for off-highway vehicles (OHVs):
- Ride only in areas you know are open to OHVs. Always respect closed areas, including designated wilderness.
- Stay on existing roads and trails; never ride or drive cross-country or make new trails.
- Don't attempt to cross or climb terrain you're not sure you can handle.
- Control your speed in areas used by others, and be prepared to stop quickly.
- Be courteous when passing others on the trail. Avoid the generation of dust and roost.

- Keep your vehicle as quiet as possible; use a silencer or muffler (and a spark arrester).
- When you encounter horses or other trail stock, stop your vehicle on the outside of the trail and shut off the engine. Take off your helmet, speak in a calm voice, and avoid sudden movements.
- Never ride without full safety equipment, or drive without using your seatbelt.

Emergency and Rescue Contacts

Dialing 911 throughout the southern Arizona area will put you in immediate contact with public safety agencies. If you need non-emergency information or assistance, the county sheriff's offices on this list are ready to help.

County Sheriff's Offices in Southern Arizona:
Cochise County
 P.O. Drawer F, Bisbee, AZ 85936 (520)432-9505
Gila County
 1100 South St., Globe, AZ 85501 (520)432-9505
Graham County
 523 10th Ave., Safford, AZ 85546 (520)428-3141
Pinal County
 140 N. Florence St., Florence, AZ 85232 (520)868-6800
Pima County
 1750 E. Benson Hwy., Tucson, AZ 85714 (520)741-4600
Santa Cruz County
 1250 N. Hohokam Dr., Nogales, AZ 85621 (520)287-4643
Yuma County
 141 S. Third Ave., Yuma, AZ 85364 (520)783-4427

Southern Arizona Rescue Association (SARA)
P.O. Box 12892, Tucson, AZ 85732 (520)295-4554
SARA is a volunteer organization composed of mountaineers and outdoors experts skilled in emergency first aid and search and rescue. SARA works in conjunction with county sheriff's departments. For volunteer information, contact them at the address and phone listed above.

Where the Trails Are: Public Lands in Southern Arizona

Southern Arizona contains more than 30,000,000 acres of land that is controlled and managed by local, state, and federal government jurisdictions. These public lands are home to some of the region's most significant natural resources—mountain ranges, riparian areas, grasslands, hill country, and more—as well as a vast array of outstanding recreational trails. This section of the *Guide* will provide you with an overview of each of these jurisdictions, the kinds of trail opportunities they offer, what makes them unique, some reading suggestions, and who you can call for more information.

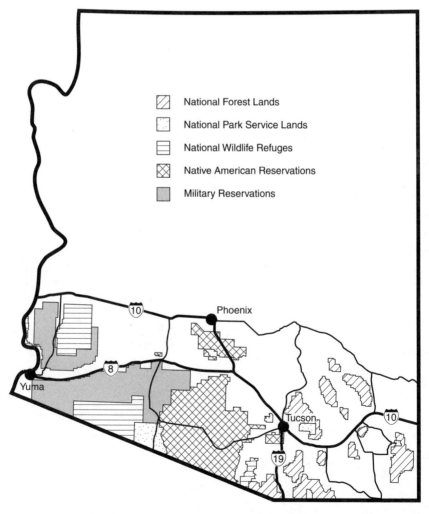

Federal Public Lands

The majority of the public lands in southern Arizona are administered by the United States government. These federal public lands include a national forest under the supervision of the **U.S. Forest Service**, national park units managed by the **National Park Service**, the **U.S. Fish and Wildlife Service**'s national wildlife refuges, and the extensive holdings of the **U.S. Bureau of Land Management**. The **U.S. Department of Defense** also controls a large amount of land in southern Arizona, some of which is open to the trail-using public. Additional information about the trail opportunities offered by these jurisdictions, including maps and guides, can be obtained by contacting the agencies directly at the numbers and addresses shown.

A Word About Wilderness

Many of the federal lands jurisdictions listed in this section contain *designated wilderness*, a special kind of public land. A wilderness area is an expanse of federally-owned property that has been set aside for careful preservation in its natural state to protect its sensitive ecosystems. Wilderness areas are established according to the principles set forth in the Wilderness Act of 1964, which defines wilderness as "...an area where the earth and its community of life are untrammeled by man, where man himself is a visitor who does not remain."

Because wilderness lands are intended to remain primitive and as pristine as possible, they are managed much more strictly than other public lands. Mechanized means of transport, including bicycles, are not allowed inside wilderness, and in most cases, mechanized maintenance equipment is forbidden. Being caught inside a wilderness area in or on a mechanized conveyance (motor vehicle or bicycle) can have serious consequences—including fines and/or jail time—so do the right thing and respect wilderness boundaries.

Twenty-eight wilderness areas are located in southern Arizona, and range from the massive and remote 803,418-acre Cabeza Prieta Refuge Wilderness to the comparatively small 2,065-acre Baboquivari Peak Wilderness southwest of Tucson. When traveling in a wilderness area on foot or horseback, keep the land's special character in mind, and do your part to preserve the solitude and wild conditions that define the *wilderness experience*.

U.S Department of Agriculture, Forest Service

Southern Arizona is home to one national forest, the 1,792,000-acre Coronado National Forest, named for the Spanish explorer Francisco Vasquez de Coronado, who explored what is now the southwestern U.S. in the early 1540s. The forest consists of five Ranger Districts, each of which is managed by a district ranger and maintains its own district office. Within each district office is at least one recreation staff member, who is the individual to contact if you have trails-related questions. This person can also provide you with any maps or trail guides the district may have produced. The Coronado National Forest is overseen by a Forest Supervisor, whose office is located at the forest's headquarters in downtown Tucson. The Coronado, like all USFS units, works to protect the diverse ecosystems under its management while providing a variety of economic and recreation opportunities. The slogan "Caring for the Land and Serving People" captures the Forest Service's mission.

Coronado National Forest
Forest Supervisor
Coronado National Forest
300 W. Congress St.
Tucson, AZ 85701
(520)670-4552

Santa Catalina Ranger District
5700 N. Sabino Canyon Rd., Tucson, AZ 85750 (520)749-8700
Fax: (520)670-4719
Website: http://www.azstarnet.com/public/nonprofit/coronado/d5home1.htm

The 262,000-acre Santa Catalina Ranger District, situated immediately north and east of Tucson, is the forest's smallest unit, but attracts its largest number of visitors because of its proximity to the city. The district encompasses the Santa Catalina Mountains, including 9,157-foot Mount Lemmon, as well as a large portion of the Rincon Mountains. With more than 400 miles of backcountry roads and trails (212 miles of trail, 195 miles of road) open to hikers, horseback riders, mountain bicyclists, and (in some areas) OHV enthusiasts, the Santa Catalina Ranger District literally has something for everyone.

Highlights of the district include a 65-mile section of the Arizona Trail, the hiking trails of the front range of the Catalinas and Rincons (Pima Canyon, Finger Rock, Pontatoc, Ventana, Milagrosa and Agua Caliente canyons), the Sabino Canyon Recreation Area, Redington Pass (a favorite riding area for mountain bikers and OHV enthusiasts), and high country trails like the Aspen Draw Trail and the Butterfly Trail. The district is served by several Pima County-managed trailhead parking facilities, which are shown on the Tucson trailheads map on page 37. Visitors to the forest must now pay a fee to use the forest's recreational facilities in the Catalina Mountains starting at Molino Basin, and a fee for access to the Sabino Canyon Recreation Area is in the works. Call the Santa Catalina Ranger District for details.

> Recommended reading:
> - *Trail Guide to the Santa Catalina Mountains*, by Eber Glendening and Pete Cowgill
> - *Tucson Hiking Guide*, by Betty Leavengood
> - *Mountain Bike Rides in the Tucson Area*, by Chris Guibert and Robert Reed

- *Mountain Biking the Old Pueblo*, by Jim Porter and Michael Jimmerson
- *Hiking Arizona's Cactus Country*, by Erik Molvar
- *Backroads and Beyond*, by Pete Cowgill

Wilderness areas in the Santa Catalina Ranger District:
- **The Pusch Ridge Wilderness**. This 56,933-acre wilderness was established in 1978 and is located at the western end of the district. Extending from the Lower Sonoran Life Zone at 2,800 feet to pine and fir forests at more than 9,000 feet, the area supports a great diversity of vegetation and wildlife, including a dwindling population of bighorn sheep. Many of this wilderness area's trails are accessible from trailheads adjacent to the Tucson metro area (see the trailheads map on page 37). The wilderness is closed to off-trail hiking from January 1 to April 30 to protect the sensitive sheep habitat. No dogs other than seeing eye or handi-dogs are allowed in the wilderness.

- **The Rincon Mountain Wilderness**. Adjacent to the east unit of Saguaro National Park, the forest's 38,590-acre Rincon Mountain Wilderness contains four life zones ranging from 3,000 feet to 7,786 feet (at Wrong Mountain). The diverse biotic communities in this wilderness support nearly 900 plant species.

Nogales Ranger District

303 Old Tucson Rd., Nogales, AZ 85621 (520)281-2296
Fax: (520)670-4598

The 370,000-acre Nogales Ranger District, the forest's third-largest unit, is located south of Tucson and encompasses most of the Santa Rita Mountains, as well as the Pajarita and Tumacacori Mountains and the grassland savannas that separate them. Its 475 miles of trails and backcountry roads (125 miles of trail, 350 miles of road) offer excellent opportunities for motorized and nonmotorized trail users alike.

The Nogales District includes Madera Canyon, a world-renowned birdwatching site that features more than 220 species of birds, as well as a 40-mile segment of the Arizona Trail that is considered to be one of the best in the state and is a special favorite of mountain bicyclists. The Arizona Trail passes through Kentucky Camp, a picturesque abandoned mining settlement established in the late 1800s. The popular Elephant Head mountain bike route, which begins southeast of Mount Hopkins and winds around the Santa Rita foothills to Madera Canyon, is also located in the district.

> Recommended reading:
> - *Hiker's Guide to the Santa Rita Mountains*, by Betty Leavengood and Mike Liebert
> - *Mountain Biking Arizona*, by Sarah Bennett
> - *Mountain Bike Rides in the Tucson Area*, by Chris Guibert and Robert Reed

Wilderness areas in the Nogales Ranger District:
- **Mount Wrightson Wilderness.** Designated in 1984, this 25,260-acre wilderness includes 9,453-foot Mount Wrightson. Key wilderness trails include the Old Baldy, Super, Crest, and Florida Canyon trails, all of which provide access to the summit.

- **Pajarita Wilderness.** The 7,420-acre Pajarita Wilderness, located approximately 15 miles west of Nogales, is accessible from the Ruby Road. The Pajarita's rugged canyons, including picturesque Sycamore Canyon, provide an important international wildlife migration corridor, and excellent hiking opportunities.

Sierra Vista Ranger District

5990 S. Highway 92, Hereford, AZ 85625 (520)378-0311
Fax: (520)670-4640

The 328,000-acre Sierra Vista Ranger District includes the Canelo Hills and the Huachuca, Patagonia, and Whetstone mountains, as well as the rolling grasslands of the beautiful San Rafael Valley. The District's 872 miles of trails and backcountry roads (140 miles of trail, 732 miles of road) includes a 55-mile stretch of the Arizona Trail, which begins on the international border within Coronado National Memorial. The Huachuca Mountains contain a variety of exceptional hiking trails, including the Crest, Sunnyside, Miller Canyon, Brown Canyon, and Hamburg trails. The Brown Canyon Trail is also popular with mountain bicyclists and equestrians, and horse corrals are available at the Ramsey Vista Campground. The South Patagonia Mountains are a favorite destination of OHV enthusiasts.

> Recommended reading:
> - *Hiker's Guide to the Huachuca Mountains (including map)*, by Leonard Taylor
> - *Hiking Arizona's Cactus Country*, by Erik Molvar

Wilderness Areas in the Sierra Vista Ranger District:
- **Miller Peak Wilderness.** This beautiful 20,190-acre wilderness overlooks the Mexican border and includes majestic 9,466-foot Miller Peak. Extensive forest fire activity has converted much of the wilderness to oak and shrub vegetation in recent years, but stands of pine and Douglas fir remain, and support more than 170 species of birds. The area is rich in mining history; many old mine sites are still visible.

Douglas Ranger District
3081 N. Leslie Canyon Rd., Douglas, AZ 85607 (520)364-3468
Fax: (520)670-4588

The 442,000-acre Douglas Ranger District is the forest's biggest unit, and includes much of the Chiricahua Mountains, the largest single mountain range in the state of Arizona. Chiricahua Peak is the highest point in the range, rising to an elevation of 9,797 feet. The rugged Dragoon Mountains, west of Sulphur Springs Valley, were once the heart of Apacheria, and include the famous Cochise Stronghold, mountain refuge for the Chiricahua Apaches. The site of Geronimo's 1886 surrender is located in the Peloncillo Mountain range in the district's southeast corner. Almost 550 miles of trails and backcountry roads exist in the district (300 miles of trail, 250 miles of road), including excellent hiking trails in all of the district's mountain ranges. The Chiricahuas include the South Fork Trail in Cave Creek (a world-class birdwatching area) and the 16-mile-long Chiricahua Crest Trail, which follows the central ridge of the range and has many connecting spurs and side loops.

> Recommended reading:
> - *Arizona Trails*, by David Mazel
> - *Hiking Trails and Wilderness Routes of the Chiricahua Mountains*, by Cachor Taylor
> - *Hiking Arizona's Cactus Country*, by Erik Molvar

Wilderness Areas in the Douglas Ranger District:
- **Chiricahua Wilderness.** First earmarked for special protection in 1933, the Chiricahua Wilderness was expanded by the 1984 Arizona Wilderness Act, and now encompasses 87,700 acres. A well-developed trail system runs through the area's rugged topography and dense forests, and adjacent forest roads provide good access to a variety of trailheads. The 27,000-acre Rattlesnake Fire of 1994 burned across much of the wilderness, changing its character for a generation of hikers. Recovery is taking place, but is a slow process.

Safford Ranger District
P.O. Box 709, Safford, AZ 85548-0709 or 504 5th Ave., Safford, AZ 85546
(520)428-4150 Fax: (520)670-4649

The 390,000-acre Safford Ranger District is home to southern Arizona's highest peak, 10,720-foot Mount Graham in the Pinaleno Mountains, as well as approximately 710 miles of trails and backcountry roads (328 miles of trail, 381 miles of road). A 29-mile-long scenic road called the Swift Trail (the first 17 miles of which are paved) leads into the high Pinalenos and provides access to campgrounds, fishing at Riggs Lake, and a wide range of outstanding forest trails. One of the most popular of these is the 32-mile Round-the-Mountain Trail on Mount Graham, which includes stands of spruce forest in the Hudsonian life zone. Mount Graham's Cunningham and Grant Hill Loop Trails are popular with mountain bicyclists.

Other "sky island" mountain ranges in the Safford District include the Galiuros, Santa Teresas, and Winchesters. The Galiuros and Santa Teresas are mostly designated wilderness. The Winchester range is small, isolated, and contains no designated trails.

Recommended reading:
- *Adventuring in Arizona*, by John Annerino
- *Hiking Arizona's Cactus Country*, by Erik Molvar
- *Travel Arizona: The Back Roads*, by James E. Cook et al

Wilderness Areas in the Safford Ranger District:
- **Galiuro Wilderness.** Designated a wilderness in 1964, the 76,317-acre area offers lots of solitude. Difficult to access, the rugged and beautiful terrain offers some outstanding trail opportunities, and colorful western history. Ten trails exist in the wilderness, including the Powers Garden, East Divide, and West Divide Trails, which offer some of the best ways to explore the area.

- **Santa Teresa Wilderness.** The 27,780-acre Santa Teresa Wilderness is located within the small but beautiful Santa Teresa Mountain Range. The Gardner Canyon, Black Rock, Cottonwood Mountain, and Holdout trails cross the area, but are poorly maintained. Road access to all trailheads is difficult; consult the forest for advice. Immediately adjacent is the BLM's 5,800-acre North Santa Teresa Wilderness.

U.S. Department of Interior, National Park Service

The National Park Service maintains seven park units in the southern Arizona region, ranging from a tiny national historic site to a large national park. Each park unit is overseen by a superintendent, with the second in command usually being the park's chief ranger. The National Park Service's approach to land management is different from that of the Forest Service and BLM, in that it seeks to balance the provision of recreational opportunities with strict natural resource preservation—an often challenging undertaking. The Park Service's trail opportunities have traditionally been limited to hiking and horseback riding, but, beginning in 1991, the agency began offering some limited trail access to mountain bicyclists.

Casa Grande Ruins National Monument

1100 Ruins Drive, Coolidge, AZ 85228 (520)723-3172
Fax: (520)723-7209

This 472-acre park houses the ruins of a massive four-story structure built by the Hohokam Indians who farmed the Gila Valley more than 600 years ago. A short self-guided nature trail provides access to the site.

Chiricahua National Monument
HCR 2, Box 6500, Dos Cabeza Route, Willcox, AZ 85643 (520)824-3560
Fax: (520)824-3421

The 11,985-acre Chiricahua National Monument is renowned for its fascinating and spectacular rock formations, which were formed by volcanic activity more than 25 million years ago. The monument, established in 1924, is home to 20 miles of terrific hiking opportunities, including the popular Echo Canyon and Heart of Rocks trails, the latter of which passes by some of the park's most famous rock formations. Equestrians have access to all park trails except for the Heart of Rocks loop, and horse staging is available in the Faraway Ranch parking area. Bikes are restricted to the park's eight miles of paved roadways. None of the trails are presently accessible to disabled users. Trail maps of the monument and the adjacent national forest are available at the visitor center. A once-daily shuttle service that transports hikers in to the backcountry leaves the visitor center at 8:30 every morning. The monument is located approximately 36 miles southeast of Willcox at the northern end of the Chiricahua Mountains.

Recommended reading:
- *Hiking Arizona's Cactus Country*, by Erik Molvar
- *Hiking Southern Arizona*, by Don R. Kiefer
- *Travel Arizona: The Back Roads*, by James E. Cook, et al
- Chiricahua National Monument Topo Map (available at the park's visitor center)
- Chiricahua Recreation Map (available at the park's visitor center)

Wilderness areas:
- **Chiricahua Monument Wilderness.** Of the monument's 11,985 acres, 10,290 acres are federally designated wilderness.

Coronado National Memorial

4101 E. Montezuma Canyon Rd., Hereford, AZ 85615 (520)366-5515 Fax: (520)366-5705

Established in 1952 to commemorate the 1540s exploration of the southwest by the Spanish explorer Francisco Vasquez de Coronado, the 4,750-acre Coronado National Memorial is located at the southern end of the Huachuca Mountains and contains approximately 9.5 miles of trails open to foot traffic only. A 3.8-mile segment of the Arizona Trail is under development through the memorial, and will provide a link from the Mexican border to the Coronado National Forest boundary. A short, steep, .5-mile interpretive trail to Montezuma Peak provides historical information about the 1540s Coronado expedition at several locations along the trail. No opportunities are offered for physically challenged users, and equestrian use is limited to the Crest Trail. Bikes are allowed only on the memorial's six miles of paved roads. The memorial's most popular hiking trails are the 3.1-mile Joe's Canyon Trail and the 3/4-mile path to Coronado Cave.

> Recommended reading:
> - *To the Inland Empire*, by Stewart Udall
> - *Travel Arizona: The Back Roads*, by James E. Cook, et al

Fort Bowie National Historic Site

P.O. Box 158, Bowie, AZ 85605 (520)847-2500 Fax: (520)847-2221

This 1,000-acre site preserves the ruins of the Fort Bowie complex, first established in 1862 as a focal point of military operations against the Apaches. Good hiking is available on a well-maintained 1.5-mile trail that gradually climbs to the fort site and passes the ruins of a Butterfield stage station, an old cemetery, and historic Apache Springs.

> Recommended reading:
> - *A Clash of Cultures*, by Robert M. Utley

Organ Pipe Cactus National Monument
Route 1, Box 100, Ajo, AZ 85321 (520)387-6849 Fax: (520)387-7661

At 330,689 acres, the Organ Pipe Cactus National Monument is the largest National Park Service unit in southern Arizona, and is filled with astounding natural beauty. The monument, located 150 miles from Tucson and adjacent to the Mexican border, is named for a species of cactus that is common in Mexico but found in the U.S. only in this area. The monument's two principal backroads, Ajo Mountain Drive and Puerto Blanco Drive, offer unpaved access to its scenic backcountry. Both of these dirt roads are popular with mountain bicyclists, who can choose between the 21-mile loop provided by the Ajo Mountain Drive, and a 53-mile loop on Puerto Blanco Drive (a segment of which follows the international border). Popular short hiking trails include the Estes Canyon–Bull Pasture and Victoria Mine trails. Horses are welcome on the monument's dirt roads and can travel cross-country, but are not allowed in developed areas (visitor center or picnic grounds) or on foot paths. Water for trail stock must be brought in. Because of the area's often extreme heat, the best months for trail use at Organ Pipe are October through April.

> Recommended reading:
> - *Adventuring in Arizona*, by John Annerino
> - *Hiking Arizona's Cactus Country*, by Erik Molvar
> - *Travel Arizona: The Back Roads*, by James E. Cook et al

Wilderness areas:
- **Organ Pipe Wilderness**. In 1978, 312,600 acres of the monument was designated a federal wilderness area.

Saguaro National Park
3693 E. Old Spanish Tr., Tucson, AZ 85730
Rincon Mountain District (East Unit): (520)733-5153 Fax: (520)733-5183
Tucson Mountain District (West Unit): (520)733-5158 Fax: (520)733-5184

Named for the majestic symbol of the Sonoran Desert—the giant Saguaro cactus—Saguaro was established as a national monument by President Hoover in 1933 and was upgraded to national park status by Congress in 1994. The park consists of two units located approximately 30 miles apart—the 67,293-acre Rincon Mountain District on the east side of the Tucson Basin, and the 24,034-acre Tucson Mountain District on the west.

The **Rincon Mountain District**, home to the park's administrative headquarters, takes in most of the Rincon Mountains, and includes life zones ranging from Lower Sonoran to Canadian. The Rincon Mountain District offers 100 miles of outstanding, scenic trails for hikers and equestrians, some of which begin on the desert floor and climb high into the Rincon Mountains (the Douglas Spring and Tanque Verde Ridge Trails). A 2.5-mile section of the Cactus Forest Trail inside the district's paved loop drive is accessible to mountain bicyclists, and was the first singletrack shared-use trail opened to mountain bikes in any U.S. National Park. Approximately

19 miles of the Arizona Trail crosses the Rincon Mountain District, via the Miller Creek (hiker route) and the Turkey Creek (equestrian route) and Italian Spring Trails. The paved .25-mile Desert Ecology Trail is wheelchair accessible. Land acquisition for the 3,500-acre expansion of the park in the Rincon Valley area southeast of Tucson is nearly complete. The expansion area is expected to offer multiple-use trail opportunities and new routes to Madrona Ranger Station, providing public access to the site for the first time since 1967. Trail maps are available at the visitor center.

The **Tucson Mountain District**, established by President Kennedy in 1961, abuts Pima County's Tucson Mountain Park and offers approximately 50 miles of trails for hikers and horseback riders. 4,687-foot Wasson Peak, the highest point in the Tucson Mountains, is a popular destination for hikers and is accessible by trail from either side of the range. Mountain bicyclists are presently confined to the district's dirt roads (the Bajada Loop Drive and Golden Gate Road), but additional opportunities are being considered. The district's first trails plan for Tucson Mountain District was recently completed, and a new trailhead parking facility providing access to the Sweetwater Trail, a popular hiking and equestrian trail, was constructed at the west end of El Camino del Cerro in 1994. Trail maps are available at the visitor center.

Recommended reading:
- *Tucson Hiking Guide*, by Betty Leavengood
- *Arizona Trails*, by David Mazel
- *Hiking Arizona's Cactus Country*, by Erik Molvar
- Saguaro National Park Map, by Trails Illustrated

Wilderness areas:
- **Saguaro Wilderness.** In 1976, Congress designated 71,400 acres of wilderness in both districts of the park—57,930 acres in the Rincon Mountain District and 13,470 acres in the Tucson Mountain District.

Tumacacori National Historical Park

P.O. Box 67, Tumacacori, AZ 85640 (520)398-2341 Fax: (520)398-9271

Located 45 miles south of Tucson and immediately east of Interstate 19, Tumacacori contains the Spanish mission sites of San Jose de Tumacacori, the Visita of San Cayetano de Calabasas, and Guevavi. A scenic 4.5-mile segment of the Juan Bautista de Anza National Historic Trail open to hikers and equestrians begins at the park, follows the Santa Cruz River, and links Tumacacori with the Tubac Presidio State Historic Park.

U.S. Department of Interior, Bureau of Land Management (BLM)

The U.S. Bureau of Land Management administers 14.2 million acres of public land in Arizona, including 12 million acres of southwestern desert, two million acres of woodlands, and more than 43,000 acres of riparian habitat. More than three million acres of the BLM's Arizona holdings are located in southern Arizona.

BLM land is managed according to the principles of multiple use and sustained yield, which means that the agency attempts to balance a wide range of recreational, commercial, scientific, and cultural interests as it strives for the long-term protection of the land's renewable and nonrenewable resources. The BLM in Arizona is organized into Field Offices, each of which is headed by a Field Office Manager. The staffs of each office usually include a recreation planner, the designated contact for trails questions. BLM lands in southern Arizona offer a wide variety of trail opportunities for all trail users, including motorized users in most cases.

BLM Arizona State Office
222 N. Central Ave., Phoenix, AZ 85004   (602)417-9200
Fax: (602)417-9399

The BLM's headquarters office for the state of Arizona is located in Phoenix. The BLM State Office operates the Arizona Public Lands Information Center (please see page 68).

BLM Field Offices in Southern Arizona

Safford Field Office
711 14th Ave., Safford, AZ 85546   (520)348-4400 Fax: (520)348-4450

The Safford Field Office administers approximately 1,383,195 acres of public land, including the following special jurisdictions:

- **Gila Box Riparian National Conservation Area** 🚶 🐎 🚵 🚙
  This special conservation area created by Congress is located 20 miles northeast of Safford and includes 15 miles of Bonita Creek and 23 miles of the Gila River. The area abounds in wildlife, including Bighorn Sheep

and over 200 species of birds. A series of primitive roads provide access throughout the area for hikers, equestrians, mountain bicyclists, and OHV users. Hiking is best in the fall, when the Gila River is running low enough to cross safely.

- **Hot Well Dunes Recreation Area**
  Hot Well Dunes is located 32 miles southeast of Safford and is one of southern Arizona's few designated OHV recreation areas. The site's 2,000 acres of rolling sand dunes are ideal for off-highway vehicle use, and are popular with All Terrain Vehicles (ATVs) and sand rail enthusiasts. Vehicles are allowed to roam anywhere within the recreation area's fenced boundary. OHV use is also permitted on the BLM property outside of the fenced area, but only on existing roads and trails. Hot Well Dunes draws its name from the artesian well that was created by an oil exploration team that struck water instead of oil on the site in the 1920s. The well that resulted flows continuously at 106 degrees, and is ideal for hot water bathing. A $3.00 fee is charged to use the site, which includes two public hot tubs, camp sites, grills, and more.

- **Black Hills Back Country Byway**
  This 21-mile backcountry route is located on a scenic dirt road that was originally a rugged pioneer route, and is recommended for high-clearance vehicles during dry weather. The byway, located between Safford and Clifton/Morenci, traverses the Black Hills area of the Peloncillo mountains and offers sweeping vistas and excellent mountain biking opportunities. Several primitive side roads that connect to the byway offer additional exploration opportunities for all trail users. Brochures describing the byway are available at the Safford Field Office.

> Recommended reading:
> - *Exploring Arizona's Wild Areas*, by Scott S. Warren

Wilderness areas:
- **Aravaipa Canyon Wilderness**
  Established in 1984, the Aravaipa Canyon Wilderness is located 25 miles southeast of Winkelman. This 19,410-acre desert riparian preserve features a rare perennial stream that runs through a steep-walled canyon. Although there are no formal trails in this wilderness, a moderately difficult 11-mile route follows the canyon bottom, with numerous stream crossings. A variety of adjacent canyons offer side trip possibilities. Hikers and equestrians must obtain an entry permit from the BLM, and there is a 50-person per day use limit. Apply for permits well in advance of your trip. Camping is allowed, but length of stay is limited to three days and two nights. Call the Safford Field Office for permits and more information.

> Recommended reading:
> - *Exploring Arizona's Wild Areas*, by Scott S. Warren
> - *Hiking Arizona's Cactus Country*, by Erik Molvar

- **North Santa Teresa Wilderness** 🚶 🐎
  This 5,800-acre wilderness created in 1990 is located approximately 25 miles west of Safford at the northeastern end of the Santa Teresa Mountains and adjoins the Santa Teresa Wilderness in the Coronado National Forest. The majority of the area consists of desert and mountain scrub, grassland, and riparian vegetation. Three poorly-maintained trails exist in the wilderness, and topo maps and a compass are strongly recommended. No public access exists to the wilderness from its north and east sides; the area must be accessed from the adjacent Coronado National Forest's Santa Teresa Wilderness.

- **Dos Cabezas Mountains Wilderness** 🚶 🐎
  This rugged desert mountain preserve seven miles south of Bowie, AZ was created in 1990 and was once an active mining area. Nearly 12,000 acres in size, the area is accessible only on its east side because of the private lands that adjoin its western boundary. No formal trails exist, but some rough four-wheel drive roads provide access to the area. Climbing 7,950-foot Cooper Peak, or 7,580-foot Government Peak, is strictly a cross-country undertaking.

- **Peloncillo Mountains Wilderness** 🚶 🐎
  Established in 1990, this wilderness is located nine miles northeast of San Simon on the border of New Mexico. The 19,440-acre area is accessible by eight short feeder roads that enter from the west and east sides of the mountain range. Most of these are rough four-wheel drive roads. An absence of formal trails means that hiking and equestrian opportunities are located in canyon bottoms or are cross-country in nature.

- **Redfield Canyon Wilderness** 🚶 🐎
  This 6,600-acre wilderness, designated in 1990, is located just south of the Coronado National Forest's Galiuro Wilderness (approximately 35 miles northwest of Willcox). Road access to the area is provided by an 18-mile-long segment of the four-wheel drive Jackson Cabin Road, which bisects the wilderness and provides access to the southern boundary of the Galiuro Wilderness. The Jackson Cabin Road can be accessed through the Nature Conservancy's Muleshoe Ranch. The area has no designated trails, but a few spur roads can be combined with cross-country travel to create hiking and equestrian opportunities.

Tucson Field Office
12661 E. Broadway Blvd., Tucson, AZ 85748 (520)722-4289
Fax: (520)751-0948

The Tucson Field Office administers approximately 750,000 acres in the south-central part of the state, including the following special jurisdictions:

- **Empire-Cienega Resource Conservation Area** 🚶 🐎 ⛰ 🚙 🏍 🏍
  This 45,000-acre preserve in southeastern Pima County and northern

Santa Cruz County just north of Sonoita includes a large quantity of Arizona State Trust Land and has been under BLM management since 1988. The Empire-Cienega's beautiful rolling grasslands offer more than 80 miles of backcountry roads and trails for all users. The area is popular with mountain bicyclists, equestrians, and OHV enthusiasts. A new segment of the Arizona Trail is expected to be sited across the Resource Conservation Area in the near future. Maps of the area are available at the Tucson Field Office and on site at a kiosk next to the main ranch road.

- **San Pedro Riparian National Conservation Area**
  1763 Paseo San Luis, Sierra Vista, AZ 85635   (520)458-3559
  Fax: (520)458-3559

  Established in 1988 to protect a 40-mile stretch of the San Pedro River, this 50,000-acre Riparian National Conservation Area is considered to be the best desert riparian area in the American Southwest. A 42-mile multi-use trail system is currently under development, and includes the 20-mile San Pedro Trail, which is open to hikers, equestrians and mountain bicyclists. A number of spur trails connect to the San Pedro Trail and provide access to various points of interest. The San Pedro features terrific scenery and outstanding birdwatching opportunities. The San Pedro House visitor center is located approximately seven miles east of Sierra Vista on State Route 90.

Wilderness areas:

- **Baboquivari Peak Wilderness**
  Located 60 miles southwest of Tucson, this wilderness was created in 1990 and derives its name from the striking 7,730-foot peak that is the focal point of the range. Located on the Tohono O'Odham Nation's eastern boundary, the wilderness covers a total of 2,065 acres. A high-clearance road accesses Thomas Canyon, where a steep, rough informal trail climbs for about four miles to a saddle just north of the peak. Hikers are rewarded with spectacular views. This trail accesses the peak, which is popular with rock climbers. The peak is also accessible from the west side of the range via a five-mile trail that begins in Baboquivari Park in the Tohono O'Odham Nation, where permits are required.

- **Coyote Mountains Wilderness**
  Established in 1990, this 5,080-acre area is located 40 miles southwest of Tucson and 6 miles east of Kitt Peak. This spectacular landscape of rugged peaks and sheer cliffs has no formal trail system. Contact the BLM Tucson Field Office for information about how to secure permission to access the wilderness across private lands.

- **White Canyon Wilderness**
  The 5,800-acre White Canyon Wilderness was designated in 1990 and is located approximately 7 miles south of Superior just off State Route 177. The area offers opportunities for hikers and equestrians to explore the beautiful stream bottom area of White Canyon, as well as a scenic

three-mile segment of the Arizona Trail. Access to the area is available via a two-wheel drive road.

Recommended reading:
- *Exploring Arizona's Wild Areas*, by Scott S. Warren
- BLM Wilderness Area Maps and Information, by U.S. Bureau of Land Management

Yuma Field Office
*2555 E. Gila Ridge Rd., Yuma AZ 85365-2240 (520)317-3200
Fax: (520)317-3250*

The Yuma Field Office administers approximately 1.5 million acres of public land in the southwestern part of the state. Much of the area's recreation opportunities are located in remote, isolated areas, and require topographical maps to access. Special features include:

- **Betty's Kitchen Interpretive Trail and Watchable Wildlife Area**
  This .5-mile fully-accessible interpretive pedestrian trail located 15 miles from Yuma provides an opportunity for visitors to learn about the Lower Colorado River ecosystem and its cultural background. The area is renowned for its outstanding birdwatching opportunities.

- **Tinajas Altas Area of Critical Environmental Concern**
  This 60,500-acre area lies close to the international border within the Barry M. Goldwater Range (see the *Guide's* U.S. Department of Defense entry on the Goldwater Range for more details). The Area of Critical Environmental Concern includes a portion of the historic El Camino del Diablo Trail, which was recently designated as a National Back Country Byway and is open to licensed OHVs, mountain bikes, equestrians, and hikers. No other formal trails exist in the area. The Area of Critical Environmental Concern offers unique pictographs, scenic vistas, and solitude. Visitors should be aware that this very isolated area requires careful trip planning and desert backcountry experience. An entry permit is required; for permit information call (520)341-2888.

- **Ehrenberg Sandbowl OHV Area**
  This 2,000-acre area was recently created to provide riding and driving opportunities for sand rails, motorcycles, ATVs, and other OHVs. The entrance to the area is located approximately two miles south of Ehrenberg, along the Colorado River.

Wilderness areas:
- **Eagletail Mountains Wilderness**
  The 100,600-acre Eagletail Wilderness, created in 1990, is located south of I-10 about 55 miles east of Quartzsite. The area's rugged buttes rise dramatically from the surrounding desert. The wilderness offers hikers lots of open terrain to explore on old jeep roads and game trails. An old vehicle route, now designated the Ben Avery Trail, bisects the wilderness, and offers hikers and equestrians more than 12 miles of quality

trail. Abandoned mining roads can be found in the Cemetery Ridge area in the southwest part of the wilderness, and offer additional opportunities for exploration.

- **Muggins Mountains Wilderness**
Located 25 miles east of Yuma, this 7,640-acre wilderness was established in 1990, and while easily accessible, the area contains no formal recreational trails. Hiking and equestrian opportunities are cross-country in nature. Rugged 1,420-foot Muggins Peak, located in the center of the wilderness in the exceptionally scenic Muggins Mountains, is a popular hiking destination.

- **New Water Mountains Wilderness**
Created in 1990, this 24,600-acre area is adjacent to and just north of the huge Kofa Refuge Wilderness. These mountains are prime Bighorn Sheep habitat. There are no formal trails in the area, but Black Mesa and Eagle Eye Arch offer interesting cross-country destinations for hikers. The best access to the area is via the Ramsey Mine Road, which begins 14 miles east of Quartzsite and south of I-10.

- **Trigo Mountains Wilderness**
This 30,300-acre area is 25 miles north of Yuma in La Paz County, and is located adjacent to the Imperial Refuge Wilderness. Created in 1990, the area is accessible only by four-wheel drive vehicle, and there are no trails. Open terrain and many washes provide a variety of hiking and horseback riding opportunities in this rugged canyon country.

> Recommended reading:
> - *Exploring Arizona's Wild Areas*, by Scott S. Warren
> - BLM Wilderness Area Maps and Information, by U.S. Bureau of Land Management

Phoenix Field Office
2015 W. Deer Valley Rd., Phoenix, AZ 85027 (602)580-5500
Fax: (602)580-5580

Most of the large quantity of land administered by the BLM's Phoenix Field Office is located north of the area covered by this **Guide**. However, the following areas of interest managed by this district are located in southern Arizona:

- **Signal Mountain Wilderness**
Located 15 miles northwest of Gila Bend, this 13,350-acre wilderness was designated in 1990. The unit is accessible from the northeast via the Agua Caliente Road, which separates it from the adjacent Woolsey Peak Wilderness to the south. No designated trails exist in the area, but several washes offer cross-country exploration opportunities. 2,182-foot Signal Peak, a popular hiking destination, is the focal point of the wilderness.

- **Woolsey Peak Wilderness**
Located immediately south of the Signal Mountain Wilderness, the most prominent feature of this 64,000-acre area is 3,270-foot Woolsey Peak. Established in 1990, the wilderness is located 11 miles northwest of Gila Bend. The area is best accessed from the Agua Caliente Road, and contains a great diversity of wildlife, including Bighorn Sheep. All travel on foot or horseback is cross country, but the terrain is not difficult.

U.S. Department of Interior, Fish and Wildlife Service

The U.S. Fish and Wildlife Service operates four National Wildlife Refuges in the southern Arizona area. The agency's mission is to conserve and manage wildlife of all kinds and the habitat necessary to support them. The U.S. Fish and Wildlife Service is also responsible for protecting and restoring populations of endangered plant and animal species.

Wildlife Management Areas in southern Arizona include:

- **Buenos Aires National Wildlife Refuge**
P.O. Box 109, Sasabe, AZ 85633 (520)823-4251 Fax: (520)823-4247

This 117,000-acre refuge was established in 1985 to provide protected habitat for the reintroduction of the Masked Bobwhite Quail. The refuge, which is home to a vast array of wildlife and over 300 species of birds, encompasses over 200 miles of backcountry roads open to motor vehicles and mountain bicyclists. Equestrians may use any of the refuge roads north of Arivaca Road. Routes in the more rugged terrain southeast of the refuge headquarters are considered ideal for mountain biking. Hiking opportunities include the many backcountry roads and the challenging five-mile (round trip) Mustang Trail, which offers solitude as well as a good hike. The area also provides opportunities for environmental studies that relate to riparian habitats, wetlands, and native and disturbed grasslands.

- **Cabeza Prieta National Wildlife Refuge**
  1611 N. Second Ave., Ajo, AZ 85321 (520)387-6483
  Fax: (520)387-5359

  Established in 1939, the 860,000-acre Cabeza Prieta Wildlife Refuge is a vast expanse of some of North America's most isolated and arid desert. There are no designated hiking trails in the refuge. Hiking opportunities are limited to cross-country travel by well-experienced desert trekkers. Two four-wheel drive roads cross the area. The El Camino Del Diablo—the "Devil's Highway"—is a 60-mile-long dirt track that crosses the southern end of the refuge, and the 18-mile route to Charlie Bell Pass traverses the Growler Mountains. Mountain bikes are allowed on four-wheel drive roads, but their use is not encouraged by the agency "...because the terrain is sandy and rocky." Horses are allowed on the refuge only with advance permission of the refuge manager. Careful preparation is a must for any excursion here; no potable water is available. All developed water sources are intended for wildlife. The air space over the Cabeza Prieta is a part of the Barry M. Goldwater Air Force Range. A permit is required to enter the refuge and an additional permit is required to enter the adjacent Goldwater Air Force Range.

Wildlife refuges:
- **Cibola National Wildlife Refuge**
  Box AP, Blythe, CA 92225 (520)857-3253

  Cibola National Wildlife Refuge is a narrow 17,000-acre jurisdiction along the Colorado River upstream from the Imperial National Wildlife Refuge. Camping is not permitted, but hiking on roads and nature trails provide opportunities for viewing wildlife, especially the Canada geese and sandhill cranes that winter here.

- **Imperial National Wildlife Refuge**
  P.O. Box 72217, Martinez Lake, AZ 85365 (520)783-3371

  Desert and river come together at this 25,125-acre refuge, which was established along the Colorado River in 1941 to protect the area's diverse plant and animal life. The refuge is located about 40 miles north of Yuma. No camping is allowed in the refuge, but the mile-long self-guided Painted Desert Trail provides an interesting and informative walk. Lookout towers are located at one-mile intervals along the main access road to provide wildlife viewing opportunities. Much of the desert foothill area along the access road is open to cross-country hiking.

- **Kofa National Wildlife Refuge**
  P.O. Box 6290, Yuma, AZ 85364 (520)783-7861 Fax: (520)783-8611

  Located approximately 40 miles north of Yuma, the 660,000-acre Kofa National Wildlife Refuge encompasses the Kofa and Castle Dome Mountains, as well as parts of the New Water, Little Horn, Tank, and Palomas Mountains. This rugged, primitive area provides seasonal habitat for a variety of wildlife including falcons and golden eagles and offers spectacular volcanic mountain and desert terrain to explore. The area is laced with approximately 300 miles of two-and four-wheel drive backcountry roads which provide access to cross-country hiking and exploring opportunities. The one-mile Palm Canyon Trail features the only native palm trees in Arizona, which are descendants of Ice Age palms. Mountain bikes are allowed on all of the refuge's backcountry roadways. Equestrians are welcome and have no travel restrictions. Check road conditions at the refuge's headquarters before setting out.

- **San Bernardino and Leslie Canyon National Wildlife Refuges**
1408 Tenth St., Douglas, AZ 85607   (520)364-2104

    Located adjacent to the San Bernardino Ranch historical area approximately 20 miles east of Douglas, the small 2,309-acre San Bernardino Refuge provides protection to endangered native fishes and other wetlands species, including over 230 varieties of birds. The nearby Leslie Canyon Refuge, located 15 miles north of Douglas, protects 1,240 acres of upland, riparian, and aquatic habitat. Both areas require permits for entry. Hiking is limited to the few dirt access roads in each area.

Wilderness areas:
- **Cabeza Prieta Refuge Wilderness**
In 1990, 803,418 acres of the refuge (93%) were set aside as federally-designated wilderness.

- **Imperial Refuge Wilderness**
In 1990, 9,220 acres of the refuge were set aside as wilderness. The BLM-managed Trigo Mountain Wilderness is immediately adjacent.

- **Kofa Refuge Wilderness**
In 1990, Arizona's Desert Wilderness Act set aside 516,300 acres of the Kofa Refuge as federal wilderness. The BLM's 24,600-acre New Water Mountain Wilderness adjoins the Kofa Wilderness on the north.

Recommended reading:
- *Adventuring in Arizona,* by John Annerino
- *Exploring Arizona's Wild Areas,* by Scott S. Warren
- *Travel Arizona: The Back Roads,* by James E. Cook et al

U.S. Department of Defense

The Department of Defense administers nearly four million acres of land in the State of Arizona, some of which is accessible to trail users for recreation purposes. Two U.S. Department of Defense units in southern Arizona that allow recreational access with the appropriate permits include:

Barry M. Goldwater Air Force Range
East Entry (602)856-3621; West Entry (520)341-3777; Cabeza Prieta National Wildlife Refuge (520)387-6483

Located south of Gila Bend, the massive 2,688,000-acre Goldwater Range is the second-largest land-based military range in the United States. One of the largest and best-preserved native desert regions in the entire southwestern U.S., this desolate area is divided into three administrative districts: the Eastern Section, managed by the U.S. Air Force; the Western Section, overseen by the U.S. Marine Corps; and the Cabeza Prieta National Wildlife Refuge, administered by the U.S. Fish and Wildlife Service. Only the Eastern and Western Sections of the range are used for ground-based military training, but the airspace over all three sections is used for air exercises. The range contains 23 mountain ranges surrounded by vast plains, and more than 1,000 miles of primitive, unimproved roads.

Permits are required for entry into each of the three districts to prevent public access during hazardous military operations. In addition, a Hold Harmless Agreement must be signed by each visitor and submitted with an entry permit application. Hiking on the range is limited to roads or cross country travel, but visitors should be aware that unexploded ordnance dating back to 1940 is scattered around the range. Mountain bicyclists and equestrians are allowed on the range, but should check with each section's headquarters for current access information. Only licensed vehicles may be operated on the range's "established-use" roadways; dirt bikes and ATVs are forbidden. Many abandoned side roads are being allowed to recover naturally, and should not be used. Camping is allowed in areas not posted as off-limits.

Fort Huachuca Military Reservation
Sierra Vista, AZ (520)533-6707 Fax: (520)538-1687

In 1877, Fort Huachuca was established as the advance headquarters for the U.S. Army's campaign against Geronimo. Today, the fort houses the Army's Information System Command and Intelligence Center. The fort encompasses more than 73,000 acres of mountain, foothill, and grassland areas. Fort Huachuca is open to the public by permit only, and visitors must present a driver's license, auto registration, and proof of insurance at the main gate to gain entrance.

Trailheads for the Garden, Huachuca and Blacktail Canyons are accessible from inside the base. Fort Huachuca borders the Sierra Vista Ranger District of the Coronado National Forest, and trails on the fort connect with trails within the forest. Garden Canyon, a popular hiking destination, provides access to several backcountry trails in the Huachuca Mountains, including the Crest Trail. The Lower and Upper Huachuca Canyon trails provide access to some beautiful higher-elevation forest trails. Camping is permitted in designated campgrounds only. For additional information, call the fort's Range Control Office at (520)533-7095.

U.S. Department of Interior, Bureau of Reclamation
P.O. Box 9980, Phoenix, AZ 85068   (602)325-5681 Fax: (602)870-6788

Another federal agency involved in the provision of recreational trail opportunities is the U.S. Bureau of Reclamation, the agency in charge of the Central Arizona Project (CAP). The right-of -way of the CAP canal will eventually be the site of a long-distance trail that will run more than 40 miles from the Tucson metro area to the Pima/Pinal county line and beyond. The first trailhead facility and 4.5 miles of the trail (from Tucson Mountain Park to the corner of Sandario and Mile Wide Roads) will be built in 1998, with additional segments to follow. The trail will be developed as a multi-use pathway, and will be open to pedestrians, mountain bicyclists, and equestrians. For additional information about the CAP Trail project, call the Pima County Parks and Recreation Department at 740-2690.

State of Arizona

Arizona State Parks
1300 W. Washington St., Phoenix, AZ 85007 (602)542-4174

Arizona State Parks is headquartered in Phoenix and maintains seven park units in the southern Arizona area that offer significant recreational trail opportunities. A permit that provides unlimited annual access to all state parks is available for $65; a *limited* access annual permit is available for $35. Fees for single-day use and camping vary according to the park and the season.

Boyce Thompson Southwestern Arboretum
37615 Highway 60, Superior, AZ 85273 (520)689-2811 Fax: (520)689-5858

The Boyce Thompson Southwestern Arboretum is a 726-acre botanical research and education center located at the base of picturesque 4,400-foot Picket Post Mountain. Founded in 1927 by copper tycoon Boyce Thompson, the arboretum is Arizona's oldest and largest public garden. Thirty-five of its 726 acres are open to the public (the remainder is reserved for research), and the park offers almost four miles of interpreted scenic nature trails that wind through a wide range of desert and exotic vegetation. The park's newest trail is the Curandero Trail, a .25 mile-long interpretive path that showcases the 25 plants traditionally used by the *curandero*, a holistic healer in the Mexican culture. The park is also known for the large variety of bird and animal species it attracts. Additional park features include picnic sites, greenhouses, and historic structures. A section of the Arizona Trail will eventually pass close by the park. A hiking trail that provides access to the top of Picket Post Mountain is located on a section of adjacent public land.

Catalina State Park
P.O. Box 36986, Tucson, AZ 85740 (520)628-5798 Fax: (520)628-5797

The 5,511-acre Catalina State Park is located in the western foothills of the Santa Catalina Mountains within the boundaries of the Coronado National Forest. The park is managed by Arizona State Parks in cooperation with the forest, and offers approximately

12 miles of trails open to hikers, equestrians, and mountain bicyclists. The park is a special favorite of horseback riders, and includes an equestrian center with horse rig parking, a corral, and other facilities. The 8-mile-long 50-Year Trail begins in the park, as do the Sutherland and Romero Canyon trails, which provide access to the forest's Santa Catalina Ranger District trail system and the Pusch Ridge Wilderness Area. The park is a popular picnic destination, has a nice nature trail, and is an excellent birdwatching site. The park also boasts a large campground facility.

Kartchner Caverns State Park
P.O. Box 1849, Benson, AZ 85602 (520)586-4110 Fax: (520)586-4123

Kartchner Caverns is a spectacular 2.5-mile-long cave complex located a short distance from Benson adjacent to the Coronado National Forest. The cave contains nearly 13,000 feet of passages, none of which had been seen by humans before the cave's discovery in 1974. A state park is being developed on the site of the cave that will include a visitor center, accessible campgrounds, picnic areas, and approximately 5 miles of nature trails—the longest of which will loop into the nearby Whetstone Mountains. Old mining and ranch roads located in the adjacent national forest will provide additional hiking, equestrian and mountain biking opportunities near the park. Because exceptional care is being taken to preserve the pristine interior of the cave, State Parks has delayed the opening to a yet-to-be-determined date.

Oracle State Park,
Center for Environmental Education
P.O. Box 700, Oracle, AZ 85623 (520)896-2425 Fax: (520)896-3215

This 4,000-acre state park and environmental education center is not yet officially open to the public, but its trail system is already being enjoyed by users from around the state. That's because the park is home to a 7-mile segment of the Arizona Trail, which is presently accessible to hikers, mountain bikers, and equestrians. The park, which is expected to open officially in 2002, will also offer two one-mile nature paths and a mile-long trail to a wildlife viewing area that connects to the Arizona Trail. Six additional miles of trails are planned for construction in the next few years.

Patagonia Lake State Park
P.O. Box 274, Patagonia, AZ 85624 (520)287-6965 Fax: (520)287-5618

The 640-acre Patagonia Lake State Park, located approximately 16 miles northeast of Nogales, is primarily a boating and camping recreation area. However, the park does include the scenic 1.2-mile (round trip) Sonoita Creek Trail, which is open to hikers. A more extensive trail system is planned for Sonoita Creek and will be implemented as funding becomes available.

Picacho Peak State Park
P.O. Box 275, Picacho, AZ (520)466-3183 Fax: (520)466-3183

The 3,600-acre Picacho Peak State Park, located approximately 40 miles north of Tucson adjacent to Interstate 10, is home to one of southern

Arizona's most prominent landmark peaks, and offers a pair of high-quality hiking opportunities—the 2-mile Hunter Trail and the 3-mile Sunset Trail. Both trails provide access to the summit of Picacho Peak, which provide spectacular views of the surrounding countryside. The two trails meet on the peak, and the final trail segment to the summit is steep and twisting. Steel cables have been anchored into the rock to help with the climb. Campsites are available at the park, but no mountain biking or equestrian opportunities are presently offered. The park is well-known for its spring wildflower displays.

Roper Lake State Park
101 E. Roper Lake Rd., Safford, AZ   (520)428-6760 Fax: (520)428-6760 (call first)

This 380-acre park located at the foot of Mount Graham features a small fishing lake with a one-mile hiking trail around the lake and a .25-mile nature trail. Less than two miles away from Roper Lake is Dankworth Pond, a State Parks facility that features a 2.5-mile hiking trail.

Tubac Presidio State Historic Park
P.O. Box 1296, Tubac, AZ 85646 (520)398-2252 Fax: (520)398-2685

Founded in 1959, the Tubac Presidio State Historic Park was Arizona's first state park, and is home to the region's original Spanish fort, or Presidio, which was established in the early 1750s. The park, which includes a museum, is located 40 miles south of Tucson just east of I-19. A scenic 4.5-mile segment of the Juan Baustista de Anza National Historic Trail open to hikers and equestrians begins near the park, and connects the Tubac Presidio with the Tumacacori National Historical Park.

Arizona State Land Department
233 N. Main Ave., Tucson, AZ 85701 (520)628-5480 Fax: (520)628-5847

The Arizona State Land Department administers 9.4 million acres of State Trust Land in Arizona, approximately 40% of which is located in southern Arizona. State Trust Lands are not public lands, and in fact have more in common with private lands. While owned by the citizens of the State of Arizona, Trust Lands exist solely to generate income for the State Trust's 14 beneficiaries, the largest of which is Arizona's school districts. All uses of State Trust Lands must benefit the Trust, which means that anyone who wants to use the land for *any* purpose—including trail use—must pay for the privilege.

Few *designated* recreational trails exist on State Trust Lands. Notable exceptions in southern Arizona are the 50-Year Trail, which begins within Catalina State Park, and several soon-to-be sited sections of the Arizona Trail in Pima and Pinal counties. However, lots of outstanding *informal* recreational trails do exist on State Trust Lands in the form of jeep and mining exploration roads, cattle trails, utility corridors, washes and more, and these opportunities can be found literally throughout the region. A good example is the large quantity of State Trust Land around the Tortolita Mountains, which is laced with old roads and trails and is popular with equestrians and mountain bicyclists. Guidebooks seldom mention these opportunities, so to locate them you'll need to rely on other users (or clubs) familiar with the area or do some exploring on your own. The *Arizona Atlas and Gazetteer's* land status maps are a good place to start. Keep in mind that most of these areas are isolated and remote, and prepare accordingly.

To facilitate the legal use of the trails that exist on its Trust Lands, the State Land Department created an annual recreational use permit, which is available from any State Land Department office for $15.00. Make sure you've secured a permit before you venture onto State Trust Lands; without it, you'll be trespassing. A new Off-Highway Vehicle recreation initiative for State Lands is under development; call the Department's program coordinator at (602)542-2926 for more information.

Recommended reading:
- *Arizona Atlas and Gazetteer,* by DeLorme Mapping
- *Backroads and Beyond,* by Pete Cowgill

Arizona Game and Fish Department

555 N. Greasewood Rd., Tucson, AZ 85745 (520)628-5376
Fax: (520)628-5080

The Arizona Game and Fish Department isn't a land manager and has no direct trails-related duties, but it does engage in a pair of important activities that are of great significance to recreational trail users. One of these activities is the conservation of wildlife and the habitat they need to survive, and the other is the department's ongoing effort to assure public access to local, state and federal lands. For additional information about the Game and Fish Department and its programs, contact the department's Tucson Office.

Local Government Jurisdictions
Pima County Parks and Recreation Department
1204 W. Silverlake Rd., Tucson, AZ 85713 (520)740-2690
Fax: (520)623-3539 Website: www.azstarnet.com/~pcpr

The Pima County Parks and Recreation Department manages six natural resource parks that offer recreational trail opportunities, as well as a river park system that provides trails in an urban setting for pedestrians, bicyclists and equestrians along several of Tucson's major watercourses. For additional information about the trails in these parks, call Pima County's trails and open space coordinator at 740-2690.

Roy P. Drachman–Agua Caliente Regional Park
12325 E. Roger Rd., Tucson, AZ 85749 (520)740-2690 Fax: (520)623-3539

Agua Caliente Regional Park is only 100 acres in size, but its unusual natural resources make it a must-see for outdoors enthusiasts. A former working cattle ranch and cavalry encampment, the park is home to a large natural hot spring that attracts a wide range of birds and animal species. An accessible .8-mile paved nature trail winds around the park and the pools produced by the spring. Several historic ranch buildings can be found on the site. The Pima County Parks and Recreation Department is presently working to secure public access to the nearby Coronado National Forest from the end of Roger Road, and if successful, the park will also serve as a staging area for hikers and mountain bicyclists (equestrians will be able to use the nearby Fort Lowell Trailhead for staging).

Cienega Creek Natural Preserve
The 3,979-acre Cienega Creek Natural Preserve, located approximately 25 miles southeast of Tucson, was established in 1986 to protect the creek's sensitive riparian ecosystem, as well as to promote natural aquifer recharge and provide flood protection for downstream Tucson. No formal trail opportunities presently exist in the preserve, but a trail system is being planned that will provide opportunities for nonmotorized trail users, and will also house a proposed segment of the Arizona Trail. The preserve attracts a wide variety of wildlife and is one of the better birdwatching areas in the Tucson area. The two trailhead parking areas for the preserve are shown on the trailheads map on page 37. Public access to the preserve is carefully controlled to help protect its fragile natural resources. A free entry permit can be obtained by calling the Pima County Parks and Recreation Department at 740-2690.

Colossal Cave Mountain Park
P.O. Box D70, Vail, AZ 85641 (520)647-7275 Fax: (520)647-3299

Colossal Cave Mountain Park is best known for the tourist attraction from which it draws its name, but this 1,800-acre natural resource park located in the picturesque southwestern foothills of the Rincon Mountains has more than just the cave to offer. The park's facilities include 2.5 miles of trails open to hikers and equestrians, as well as picnic and camp sites. A future expansion of the park will include the development of additional trail opportunities, including a link down the Agua Verde Creek corridor to the Cienega Creek Natural Preserve that will house a future segment of the Arizona Trail.

Pima Motorsports Park
Harrison Rd. between Brekke Rd. and Dawn Rd. (520)740-2690
Fax: (520)623-3539

Pima Motorsports Park is a 640-acre off-highway vehicle (OHV) park located west of the Pima County Fairgrounds within the county's 2,350-acre Southeast Regional Park. The park, which is now under development and is expected to open in 1999, will offer a variety of riding and driving opportunities for motorcycles, ATVs, go-karts, and four-wheel drive vehicles. Facilities will include a rider/driver training area, a classroom/administration building, several motocross and ATV tracks (including a children's track), a paved kart track, a 4x4 obstacle course, and more. A BMX track is also planned for the site, and the park's facilities may also be shared with mountain bicyclists on a special-event basis.

Tortolita Mountain Park
In 1986 and 1987, Pima County acquired 3,056 acres of land in the Tortolita Mountains with the intention of eventually developing the holding into a natural resource park. Access to the now 3,245-acre property is presently restricted, but the park's master planning process has been completed, and the acquisition of public access and the construction of roads, trails, and trailhead facilities will occur within the next few years using bond funding approved by Pima County voters in May, 1997. A plan to expand the park by adding adjacent BLM and Arizona State Trust Land is also in the works. The park's future (40.5 mile) trail system will offer outstanding opportunities for hikers, equestrians, and mountain bicyclists.

Tucson Mountain Park
The 21,000-acre Tucson Mountain Park is located on the west side of the Tucson metro area and offers 26 miles of terrific desert trails for hikers, equestrians, and mountain bicyclists. The park, established in 1928, is a particular favorite of mountain bicyclists, the park's largest user group. Popular hiking opportunities include the picturesque David Yetman Trail, the Golden Gate Trail, and the Brown Mountain Trail. Tucson Mountain Park's trailheads are shown on the trailheads map on page 37. Amenities include picnic sites, a scenic overlook at Gates Pass, and overnight camping at the Gilbert Ray campground. Old Tucson, a western theme park, and the world-renowned Arizona-Sonora Desert Museum are located within the park. A large trails map of Tucson Mountain Park can be purchased for $3.00 at the Pima County Parks and Recreation Department. Tucson Mountain Park is closed to OHV use. Park hours are from 7 A.M. to 10 P.M. Alcoholic beverages and firearms are not permitted.

Recommended reading:
- *Tucson Hiking Guide*, by Betty Leavengood
- *Mountain Bike Rides in the Tucson Area*, by Chris Guibert and Robert Reed

Pima County River Park System

Pima County is in the process of developing a system of river park trails that follow the Tucson metro area's principal watercourses. To date, 8 miles of trails have been completed along the east and west banks of the Santa Cruz River. Both banks are open to bicycle and pedestrian use; equestrians use the bed of the river. 7.5 miles have been completed along the Rillito River. The south bank trail is for pedestrian and equestrian use only, and the north bank is for pedestrians and bicycles. Equestrians also use the bed of the Rillito. An expansion of the Rillito River park now underway will extend the park east to Craycroft Road and west to the Santa Cruz River. Three new trailhead facilities are a part of the expansion project. Two will be located at the Rillito's intersection with Swan Road, with one of these serving equestrian users. One will be at the intersection of Camino de la Tierra and the Rillito.

Future river park development will include the Cañada del Oro Wash, the Tanque Verde Creek, and the Pantano Wash, which will help link Tucson's urban core to the public lands that surround the city. A map of river park trail segments now in place, the trailheads that serve them, and river park segments planned for the near future can be found below.

Recommended reading:
- Pima County River Parks Master Plan, by Pima County Department of Transportation and Flood Control District

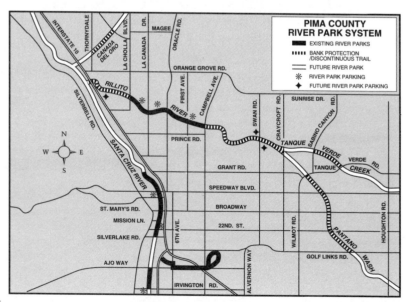

Trailheads in the Tucson Metro Area

Access to the trails that exist within the public lands jurisdictions that surround Tucson is readily available from a variety of public trailhead parking facilities. The trailheads map below shows where these facilities are located. Pertinent details about each trailhead and the trails they provide access to is listed on the following pages.

Trailhead Tips:
Trailhead parking capacity is limited; carpool whenever possible.
Trailheads usually fill up quickly; arrive early to secure a space.
Parking outside of designated trailhead areas may result in your vehicle being ticketed. Be sure to obey all posted signage, particularly *No Parking* signs along access roads.

As in all remote areas where you park your car, secure your valuables out of sight or, better yet, take them with you for safe keeping.

Pima County-managed trailheads (marked with an *) open at 5 A.M. and close at 9 P.M., except as otherwise noted. Note that trailhead hours may vary according to location and managing agency.

Important Note: Parking in all Pima County-managed trailheads after hours or overnight requires a **trailhead parking permit** (available for a one-time fee of $10). Call the Pima County Parks and Recreation Department at 740-2690 for details.

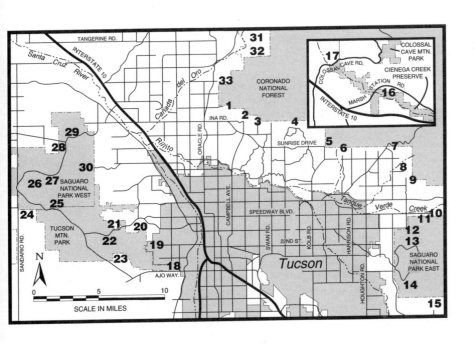

37

Trailheads

1 **Pima Canyon*** 🚶

This 44-car lot provides access to the Pima Canyon Trail in the Coronado National Forest, one of the most popular and scenic in southern Arizona. The lot and first 1,700 feet of the trail are owned by Pima County. Dogs are not allowed on the trail. Open 5 A.M. to 9 P.M. Details: (520)740-2690 (Pima County) or (520)749-8700 (Coronado National Forest).

2 **Campbell*** 🚶

A small paved parking area maintained by Pima County at the northern end of Campbell Boulevard, the Campbell Trailhead connects to an unattractive fenced corridor that provides general access to the Coronado National Forest, but not to a designated trail. Open 5 A.M. to 9 P.M. A Pima County permit ($10 one-time fee) is required to park here after 9 P.M. Details: (520)740-2690 (Pima County) or (520)749-8700 (Coronado National Forest).

3 **Finger Rock*** 🚶

A 31-car lot at the northern end of Alvernon Way provides access to the Finger Rock, Pontatoc Ridge, and Pontatoc Canyon Trails in the Coronado National Forest. This very popular trailhead fills quickly on weekends and holidays. Open 5 A.M. to 9 P.M. Details: (520)740-2690 (Pima County).

4 **Ventana Canyon*** 🚶

The Ventana Trailhead is located at the back of the Ventana Canyon Resort's employee parking area and has space for 25 cars. A 5,200-foot-long county-controlled access trail, most of which follows the Ventana Wash, connects the trailhead with the forest. Dogs are not allowed on this trail. Open 5 A.M. to 9 P.M. Details: (520)740-2690 (Pima County).

5 **Sabino Canyon Recreation Area** 🚶 🚴

The parking lot of the Sabino Canyon Recreation Area provides an excellent staging point for many popular hiking trails in the front range of the Catalina Mountains, including Blackett's Ridge Trail, Esperero Trail, Seven Falls Trail, Phone Line Trail, Bear Canyon Trail, and the Sabino Canyon Trail—all of which provide access to the forest's backcountry trail system. The lot is large but fills quickly on weekends and holidays. Check with the Forest Service as to restrictions on bike use in this area. Open 24 hours. Details: (520)749-8700 (Coronado National Forest).

6 **Bear Canyon*** 🚶 🚴

This primitive dirt parking area is located alongside the Bear Canyon Road right-of-way near its northern end and has room for about 10 cars. Users can follow the undeveloped county dirt road bed north a short distance to access to the Bear Canyon area of the Coronado National Forest and the Bear Canyon Trail. Bicyclists are not permitted beyond end of road where trail enters wilderness area. Open 5 A.M. to

9 P.M. Details: (520)740-2690 (Pima County) or (520)749-8700 (Coronado National Forest).

7 Avenida de Suzenu* 🚶 🐎

This staging area is actually side-of-the-road parking at the northern end of Avenida de Suzenu, a residential dirt road in the far northeast corner of the Tucson Basin. Hikers and equestrians must pass through a gate and walk east down private Horsehead Road to get to the forest boundary. This route provides access to the Agua Caliente region of the forest and its trail system, as well as scenic Agua Caliente and Milagrosa Canyons. Open 5 A.M. to 9 P.M. Details: (520)740-2690 (Pima County) or (520)749-8700 (Coronado National Forest).

8 Agua Caliente Park* 🚶 🚴

The public parking lot on the park's east end doubles as a staging area for access to the Agua Caliente area of the Coronado National Forest for hikers and mountain bikers (equestrians can stage at the nearby Agua Caliente Hill South Trailhead—see below). Forest access from the end of adjacent Roger Road is under negotiation; call for status. Open park hours are 7 A.M. to sunset. Details: (520)740-2690 (Pima County).

9 Agua Caliente Hill South* 🚶 🐎 🚴

Presently a small dirt clearing near the end of Camino Cantil, a residential street accessible from the east end of Fort Lowell Road, this trailhead is expected to become a 16-car, 4-horse rig paved parking lot in late 1998, and will provide access to the Coronado National Forest's Agua Caliente trail system. Open 5 A.M. to 9 P.M. Details: (520)740-2690 (Pima County) or (520)749-8700 (Coronado National Forest).

10 Douglas Spring 🚶

This small parking lot at the end of East Speedway Boulevard has room for 16 cars and provides access to the Cactus Forest Trail system and the popular Douglas Spring Trail in Saguaro National Park East. The lot is for hikers only; equestrian staging is located alongside Speedway Boulevard a short distance to the west at the Wildhorse Gate (see below). Open 24 hours. Details: (520)733-5153 (Saguaro National Park East).

11 Wildhorse Gate 🐎

The Wildhorse Gate is Saguaro National Park East's designated equestrian staging area for the Cactus Forest Trail system near the end of East Speedway Boulevard.

Horse rigs can park along both shoulders of the road, with room for about 10 rigs on each side. Be sure to park entirely off the paved roadway. Details: (520)733-5153. Open 24 hours. (Saguaro National Park East).

12 Broadway Gate 🚶

The Broadway Gate is the access point to Saguaro National Park's Cactus Forest Trail system from the end of East Broadway Boulevard. Trail users must park alongside the road at present, but a new trailhead is planned. Capacity exists for about 12 cars. Be sure to park entirely off of the paved roadway. Open 24 hours. Details: (520)733-5153 (Saguaro National Park East).

13 Loma Verde 🚶

The Loma Verde trailhead is located within Saguaro National Park East adjacent to the park's Cactus Forest Drive, has space for 7 cars, and provides hiking access to the Cactus Forest Trail system. Open 7 A.M. to sunset. Details: (520)733-5153 (Saguaro National Park East).

14 Tanque Verde Ridge 🚶

Parking for 10 cars is located within Saguaro National Park East's Javelina Picnic Area for the Tanque Verde Ridge Trail. Staging is for hikers only; stock is not allowed on the trail. Details: (520)733-5153 (Saguaro National Park East).

15 Camino Loma Alta 🚶 🐎 🚴

A temporary parking area has been established by Saguaro National Park at the northern end of Camino Loma Alta to provide access to the park's newly-acquired 3,500-acre expansion area and its informal trail system. Unpaved parking is available for about 10 cars; an improved lot is planned. Open 24 hours. Details: (520)733-5153 (Saguaro National Park East).

16 Davidson* 🚶 🐎

This 10-car, 6-horse rig paved lot just off of Marsh Station Road a short distance west of Three Bridges (watch for signs) provides access to the Cienega Creek Natural Preserve and Davidson Canyon. **Note:** A permit is required to access the preserve. Open 5 A.M. to 9 P.M. Details: (520)740-2690 (Pima County).

17 Colossal Cave Road* 🚶 🐎 🚴

An undeveloped dirt parking area south of Colossal Cave Road at the northern end of the Cienega Creek Preserve, this trailhead has room for approximately 10 cars and 2 horse rigs and provides access to the preserve. A paved lot is planned. Note: A permit is required to access the preserve. Open 5 A.M. to 9 P.M. Details: (520)740-2690 (Pima County).

18 Explorer 🚶 🚴

The Explorer Trailhead is located at the back of the City of Tucson's Kennedy Park Fiesta Area parking lot, which is accessible from La Cholla Boulevard. The lot is large, but can fill during special events. The lot provides access to Tucson Mountain Park's Explorer Trail. Open 7 A.M. to 10 P.M. Details: (520)740-2690 (Pima County).

19 Starr Pass East*

A primitive dirt parking area located adjacent to the Starr Pass development and CAP reservoir at the end of a rough dirt access road, this trailhead has room for 20 cars and 6 horse rigs. The trailhead provides access to the Starr Pass Trail and Tucson Mountain Park trail system, and is the designated equestrian staging area for Tucson Mountain Park. Details: (520)740-2690 (Pima County).

20 David Yetman East*

This tiny dirt lot located at the southern end of Camino de Oeste near the Tucson Mountain Park boundary has room for 5 cars, and provides access to the Tucson Mountain Park's David Yetman Trail. (Equestrian staging for Tucson Mountain Park is located at the Starr Pass East Trailhead). Open 7 A.M. to 10 P.M. Details: (520)740-2690 (Pima County).

21 Gates Pass*

This paved staging area is located within Tucson Mountain Park's Gates Pass Overlook, has space for 50 cars, and serves the Gates Pass Trail. Equestrian staging for Tucson Mountain Park is located at the Starr Pass East Trailhead. Open 7 A.M. to 10 P.M. Details: (520)740-2690 (Pima County).

22 David Yetman West*

A paved lot located just off Gates Pass Road on the west side of the pass at the bottom of the hill, this trailhead has space for 12 cars and provides access to Tucson Mountain Park's David Yetman Trail. Equestrian staging for Tucson Mountain Park is located at the Starr Pass East Trailhead. Open 7 A.M. to 10 P.M. Details: (520)740-2690 (Pima County).

23 Sarasota*

A 20-space trailhead is planned for the end of Sarasota Road adjacent to Tucson Estates that will provide access to the west end of the Starr Pass Trail in Tucson Mountain Park. Equestrian staging for Tucson Mountain Park is located at the Starr Pass East Trailhead. Open 7 A.M. to 10 P.M. Details: (520)740-2690 (Pima County).

24 Central Arizona Project (CAP)*

When built in late 1998, the CAP Trailhead will be located near the southeast corner of the intersection of Sandario and Mile Wide Roads within the Central Arizona Project corridor, and will have space for 18 cars (with one accessible space) and 5 horse rigs. The trailhead will serve a 4.5-mile shared-use segment of the CAP Trail that will link the trailhead to Tucson Mountain Park. Open 5 a.m to 9 P.M. Details: (520)740-2690 (Pima County).

25 King Canyon*

This primitive dirt lot across Kinney Road from the Arizona–Sonora Desert Museum is located within Tucson Mountain Park, but serves the King Canyon Trail in Saguaro National Park West, as well as Tucson Mountain Park's planned Cougar Trail. Note: Bikes are not allowed on Saguaro West trails. Space exists for roughly 15 cars and 3 horse rigs. The lot fills quickly, especially during the cooler months. Open 7 A.M. to 10 P.M. Details: (520)740-2690 (Pima County) or (520)733-5158 (Saguaro National Park West).

26 Hugh Norris 🚶

This trailhead situated within Saguaro National Park West just off the unpaved Bajada Loop Drive has room for 8 cars, and provides access to the Hugh Norris Trail. The lot is for hikers only; horses are prohibited on the Hugh Norris Trail. Open 6 a.m to sunset. Details: (520)733-5158 (Saguaro National Park West).

27 Sendero Esperanza 🚶

The Sendero Esperanza Trailhead is located adjacent to Golden Gate Road in the heart of Saguaro National Park West roughly 2.5 miles south of Picture Rocks Road. It has space for 10 cars, and provides access to the Sendero-Esperanza Trail. Open 6 A.M. to sunset. Details: (520)733-5158 (Saguaro National Park West).

28 Cam-Boh Picnic Area 🚶 🐎

Informal dirt-lot staging for 6 cars and 2 horse rigs is available at this Saguaro National Park West facility located just south of Picture Rocks Road. The trailhead provides access to the Cam-Boh Trail. Open 24 hours. Details: (520)733-5158 (Saguaro National Park West).

29 Box Canyon 🚶 🐎

A primitive dirt lot within Saguaro National Park West located immediately north of Picture Rocks Road with room for 5 cars and 3 horse rigs, this trailhead connects to the Box Canyon, Cam-Boh and Ringtail trails. Open 24 hours. Details: (520)733-5158 (Saguaro National Park West).

30 El Camino del Cerro* 🚶 🐎

This 10-car, 2-horse rig paved trailhead is located at the western end of El Camino del Cerro and provides access to the popular Sweetwater Trail and other trails in Saguaro National Park's West Unit. Open 5 A.M. to 9 P.M. Details: (520)740-2690 (Pima County) or (520)733-5158 (Saguaro National Park West).

31 Catalina State Park 🚶 🐎 🚵

Catalina State Park has a single large trailhead with space for 150 cars that provides access to the park's nature and birding trails, as well as the shared-use 50 Year Trail, the Canyon Loop Trail, and the trail system on the adjacent Coronado National Forest, which includes the popular Romero Canyon and Sutherland Trails. Overnight parking is permitted for a fee of $8 for the first night and $4 for each additional night. Equestrian staging is available at the park's equestrian center (see below). Open 5 A.M. to 10 P.M. Details: (520)628-5798 (Catalina State Park).

32 **Catalina State Park Equestrian Center**
One of the few equestrian centers in the Tucson Basin is located here, and its large dirt lot has room for about 30 horse rigs. The center links to the park's bridle trail, the shared-use 50 Year Trail, and trails in the Coronado National Forest. Corrals and water are available, as are picnic sites, grills, and more. Camping is available for a fee. Open 5 A.M. to 10 P.M. Details: (520)628-5798 (Catalina State Park).

33 **Linda Vista***
A small paved lot with room for 6 cars is located just off East Linda Vista Road near the boundary of the Coronado National Forest, and provides access to the forest's Linda Vista Trail. Horse staging is not available here, but equestrians are welcome on the trail, which leads into the Pusch Ridge Wilderness area. Open 5 A.M. to 9 P.M. Details: (520)740-2690 (Pima County) or (520)749-8700 (Coronado National Forest).

City of Yuma

3 W. Third St., Yuma, AZ 85364 (520)783-1277 Fax: (520)343-8707
The City of Yuma is presently planning a system of linear parks that will follow the community's major watercourses and will provide opportunities for bicyclists and pedestrians. For additional information, call the Planning and Neighborhood Services Division of the city's Department of Community Development at the number listed above.

Barrier-Free Facilities ♿

Little more than a decade ago, outdoor facilities that made provisions for physically challenged users were virtually unknown. Today, a variety of accessible facilities exist, and the number is continuing to grow, thanks to the Americans with Disabilities Act (ADA) and the sensitization of public agencies to the needs of disabled recreationists. The following list provides some examples of barrier-free trails and trails-related facilities that can be found in the southern Arizona area. To locate additional opportunities, we recommend the following guides: *Access Arizona, An Atlas and Travel Guide for Disabled and Mature Travelers to Major Outdoor Recreation Areas*, and *Recreation Guide to Barrier-Free Facilities—Southwestern National Forests*. Information about both of these books is located in the Publications section of this *Guide*.

Agua Caliente Regional Park
This 100-acre county park on Tucson's far northeast side features a large natural hot springs and a .8-mile accessible nature trail. Additional accessible trails may be added in the future. Details: (520)740-2690 (Pima County Parks and Recreation).

Betty's Kitchen Interpretive Trail and Watchable Wildlife Area
A .5-mile interpretive trail located on BLM land about 15 miles from Yuma, the Betty's Kitchen Trail provides an opportunity for visitors to learn about the Lower Colorado River ecosystem and features accessible walkways, parking, restrooms, and a fishing pier. All of the trail's nine interpretive exhibits are also accessible. Details: (520)726-6300 (Yuma Field Office BLM).

CAP Trail and Trailhead
The first 4.5-mile section of the natural-surface CAP Trail will be developed with accessibility in mind, as will its trailhead facility. The trailhead, which will be built west of Tucson Mountain Park at the corner of Sandario and Mile Wide Roads in late 1998, will feature a special ramp that will make it easier for physically challenged equestrians to mount their horses. Details: (520)740-2690 (Pima County Parks and Recreation).

East Cochise Stronghold Campground
Located in a rugged canyon in the Dragoon Mountains in the Coronado National Forest, this site includes barrier-free parking, picnic sites and restrooms, as well as two nature trails that offer varying degrees of accessibility. Details: (520)364-3468 (Douglas Ranger District, Coronado National Forest).

Madera Canyon Recreation Area
One of the world's best birdwatching sites, the Madera Canyon Recreation Area, located on the west side of the Santa Rita Mountains in the Nogales Ranger District of the Coronado National Forest, also offers barrier-free parking, picnic sites, restrooms, and a 1.5-mile paved trail system. Details: (520)281-2296 (Nogales Ranger District, Coronado National Forest).

Parker Canyon Lake Recreation Area
Situated in the rolling Canelo Hills south of Sonoita, this recreation area boasts an accessible parking area, boat launch, fishing pier, and paved Lakeshore Trail. The trail offers exceptional opportunities to observe wildlife. Details: (520)378-0311 (Sierra Vista Ranger District, Coronado National Forest).

Pena Blanca Lake Recreation Area
A forest recreation area located northwest of Nogales, Pena Blanca includes accessible picnic areas, ramadas, restrooms, and the 1,300-foot Pena Blanca Lakeshore Trail, which provides access to a floating fishing pier. Details: (520)281-2296 (Nogales Ranger District, Coronado National Forest).

Pima County River Park Trails
Both the Santa Cruz River Park and the Rillito River Park offer paved trails on level ground within metro Tucson. Barrier-free parking lots for the Rillito River Park are located south of River Road between La Cholla Boulevard and La Canada Drive, on the north bank of the park at Swan Road, and at the Rillito Racetrack east of First Avenue. Accessible lots for the Santa Cruz River Park can be found on the east bank just north of 22nd Street, on the west bank just east of Irvington Road, and on the west bank at Speedway Boulevard. Expansion of both of these linear parks, as well as the development of several others, is planned for the near future. Details: (520)740-2690 (Pima County Parks and Recreation).

Sabino Canyon Recreation Area
About three-quarters of a mile of the Sabino Canyon Recreation Area's paved road system is easily accessible to physically challenged users, and provides access to a variety of points of interest, including the new visitor center. A .5-mile nature trail will be accessible as soon as a new culvert has been installed near its trailhead. A motorized tram that runs year 'round ferries visitors to the upper reaches of the canyon. Details: (520)749-8700 (Santa Catalina Ranger District, Coronado National Forest).

Where the Trails Are: Other Lands in Southern Arizona

Besides the many acres of public land in the region there are two other kinds of lands that provide excellent trail opportunities. The Tohono O'Odham Nation, which covers a vast area, currently allows public hiking access to a small but very exceptional area in the Baboquivari Mountains. The Nature Conservancy, which manages lands comprising more than 58,000 acres in Southern Arizona, provides hikers with opportunities to experience many unique ecosystems first hand.

Tribal Jurisdictions
Tohono O'Odham Nation 🚶

Baboquivari District - P.O. Box 3001, Sells, AZ 85634 (520)383-2366

The 2,800,000-acre Tohono O'Odham Nation is as big as the state of Connecticut, and the second-largest reservation in the United States. The nation offers one designated recreational trail opportunity, the 5.5-mile Baboquivari Peak Trail, which begins at the western base of the peak in Baboquivari Park. The trail is steep with many switchbacks, and provides outstanding vistas. The peak is also a popular rock climbing destination. A fee permit to use the trail must be obtained from the Baboquivari District Office in Topawa, eight miles south of Sells.

Recommended reading:
- *Adventuring in Arizona*, by John Annerino

Nature Conservancy Preserves

The Nature Conservancy is an international nonprofit conservation organization that seeks to preserve rare and significant plant and animal species by protecting the habitats they need to survive. The Conservancy owns and manages 1,400 preserves worldwide, including ten in Arizona. Five of the Conservancy's Arizona preserves that are open to the public are located in southern Arizona.

The Nature Conservancy – Arizona Field Office
300 E. University Blvd., Ste. 230 Tucson, AZ (520)622-3861
Fax: (520)620-1799 Website: www.tnc.org

The Conservancy's headquarters for the state of Arizona is located in Tucson. Literature describing the Conservancy's programs and each of its preserves is available at this office.

Aravaipa Canyon Preserve
(520)828-3443
The 7,000-acre Aravaipa Canyon Preserve is located at both ends of the U.S. Bureau of Land Management's Aravaipa Canyon Wilderness, and access to the wilderness is routed through the preserve. No formal trails exist within the preserve; most visitors come to hike the BLM's beautiful 11-mile-long canyon, which boasts perennial stream flow and lush vegetation. The preserve attracts a wide variety of animal life, including over 200 species of birds. Hikers and equestrians are allowed into the wilderness only with a permit from the BLM. Permits are available through the BLM's Safford Field Office at (520)348-4400; advance reservations are required.

Canelo Hills Preserve
P.O. Box 815, Patagonia, AZ 85624 (520)394-2400
Located just off State Highway 83 south of Sonoita, this preserve consists of 260 acres of wetlands surrounding O'Donnell Creek. A rare orchid, many birds and scenic beauty make this mini-wilderness an interesting destination. An easy 1.5-mile hiking trail allows exploration of the area.

Muleshoe Ranch Preserve
RR1, Box 1542, Willcox, AZ 85643 (520)586-7072
Located in the foothills of the Galiuro Mountains approximately 35 miles northwest of Willcox, this 49,080-acre preserve is composed of Conservancy, Forest Service and BLM lands. The ranch offers trail opportunities for hikers and equestrians, including the 5.5-mile (hiker-only) Beth Woodin Trail, and the High Lonesome Trail, part of a 14-mile loop. Equestrians must call ahead for permission to stage at the ranch. Mountain biking and four-wheel drive opportunities are available on the adjacent Jackson Cabin Road, which provides access to the south boundary of the Galiuro Wilderness. Overnight accommodations are available in casitas or in a campground. Call for hours of operation.

Patagonia-Sonoita Creek Preserve 🚶
P.O. Box 815, Patagonia, AZ 85624 (520)394-2400
Established in 1966, this 1,165-acre preserve was the first Conservancy project in Arizona. The area protects some of the richest remaining riparian habitat in the region. Over 260 species of birds can be observed here. The easy 1.6-mile Sonoita Creek Loop Trail (hiking only) partly follows an old railroad bed and traverses floodplain and riparian habitats. This preserve has variable hours—call ahead.

Ramsey Canyon Preserve 🚶
27 Ramsey Canyon Rd., Hereford, AZ 85624 (520)378-2785
This 300-acre preserve is located within Ramsey Canyon on the eastern flank of the Huachuca Mountains next to the Coronado National Forest. The area is renowned for its scenic beauty and its 170 species of birds, including 14 varieties of hummingbirds. The 10-mile-long Ramsey Canyon Loop begins in the preserve and continues into the forest, providing a moderately difficult hike to the crest of the Huachuca range and the Miller Peak Wilderness. Limited day parking and overnight accommodations are available; call for reservations and preserve hours.

A Note About Private Lands

While most of the recreational trails in southern Arizona are located on public lands, many popular trails—especially in urban areas—cross private property at some point or pass in close proximity to it. Private landowners can be a trail user's best friend or worst nightmare, so always remember to respect their rights and feelings as you go about your business. Never trespass on posted lands. Secure permission to enter private property before you hike or ride. Be sure to close gates behind you, and pass by homes *quietly*. Keeping private landowners happy will help protect our precious, hard-won trail access, and keep us all enjoying trails for years to come.

Trail Projects, Programs, and Events

The Arizona Trail

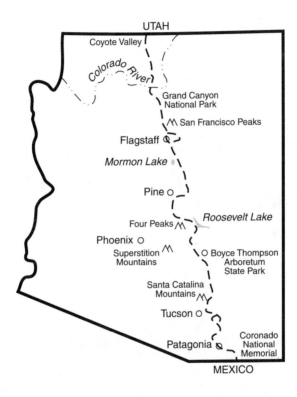

Arizona's preeminent long-distance recreational trail is the Arizona Trail, a nonmotorized shared-use opportunity that has been under development since 1985. When finished around the turn of the century, the trail, which incorporates some of the state's best existing recreational trails, will span the state from Utah to Mexico, a distance of some 780 miles. 400 miles of the trail are now complete, and offer a variety of outstanding opportunities for hikers, equestrians, and mountain bicyclists (outside of wilderness areas). The development of the Arizona Trail is being coordinated by Arizona State Parks, which created the position of *Arizona Trail Steward* to manage the project. For additional information about the Arizona Trail project, call the Arizona Trail Steward at (602)542-4174, or write c/o Arizona State Parks, 1300 W. Washington St., Phoenix, AZ 85007.

In 1993, the nonprofit **Arizona Trail Association** (ATA) was formed to help public agencies complete the trail by the year 2000. The ATA is composed entirely of volunteers, and serves many important functions, including working with land agencies and landowners to site the trail, organizing trail building and trail maintenance projects, raising funds to pay for signs and new trail construction, and much more. To find out how you can become a member of the ATA, or to receive information about Arizona Trail volunteer opportunities, contact the association at P.O. Box 36736, Phoenix, Arizona 85067; (602)252-4794.

Some of the best of the trail's 34 segments are located in southern Arizona. The *Guide*'s Arizona Trail map on page 49 shows the trail location in Arizona. Several major publishers are now preparing guidebooks for the trail, the first of which should be available in the fall of 1998. Arizona Trail "Passage Sheets," which provide a map and information about the trail, are available for some of the trail's completed segments from the Arizona Trail Association and Arizona State Parks.

> Recommended reading:
> - Arizona Trail Management Guide, by Arizona State Parks

Completed Segments of the Arizona Trail in Southern Arizona

Approximately 165 miles of the Arizona Trail have been completed in the southern Arizona area. Public agencies, the Arizona Trail Association and local trails groups are hard at work to locate and complete the remaining 90 miles by the year 2000. The Arizona Trail segments that are presently open and ready to use are listed below. For more information about these segments, call the number shown for each entry, or contact the Arizona Trail Steward at (520)542-7120.

Segment 1   Coronado National Memorial
Details: (520)366-5515
The Arizona Trail is complete across the Coronado National Memorial from the Mexican border to the memorial's boundary with the Coronado National Forest, a total distance of 3.75 miles. This section of the trail is presently open to hikers and equestrians only.

Segment 2   Huachuca Mountains
Details: (520)378-0311
Located in the Sierra Vista Ranger District of the Coronado National Forest, this 19.4-mile segment, which opened in 1989, begins at the northern boundary of the Coronado National Memorial and stretches to Forest Road 194 near Parker Canyon Lake. Most of this segment (13.1 miles) is located in the Miller Peak Wilderness. Mountain bikers can take an alternate route on Forest Roads 61/48.

Segment 3	**Canelo Hills East**
	Details: (520)378-0311

This 14.5-mile segment of the trail from Forest Road 194 (near Parker Canyon Lake) to Forest Road 799 (near Canelo Pass) has been finished since 1993 and is open to hikers, equestrians and mountain bikers.

Segment 4	**Canelo Hills West**
	Details: (520)378-0311

This 18.9-mile segment of the trail begins at Forest Road 799 near Canelo Pass and ends at the Harshaw Trailhead at the forest boundary. This segment was completed in 1995 and is open to hikers, equestrians and mountain bikers.

Segment 6	**South Santa Rita Mountains**
	Details: (520)281-2296

This 26.7-mile segment begins on Forest Road 72 at the Coronado National Forest Nogales Ranger District boundary and terminates near Kentucky Camp. Completed in 1994, the trail winds through the scenic Santa Rita Mountains. The trail is especially popular with mountain bicyclists who are allowed to use all but a 2.2-mile section (the Walker Basin Trail) that passes through the Mount Wrightson Wilderness.

Segment 7	**North Santa Rita Mountains**
	Details: (520)281-2296

This 13.3-mile segment that begins at Kentucky Camp in the Nogales Ranger District of the Coronado National Forest and ends at the forest's boundary with the BLM's Empire-Cienega Resource Conservation Area near Oak Tree Canyon. This popular segment is open to hikers, equestrians and mountain bikers.

Segment 13	**Redington Pass**
	Details: (520)749-8700

This 17.7-mile segment is entirely located in the Santa Catalina Ranger District of the Coronado National Forest. It begins on the Italian Spring Trail at the northern boundary of Saguaro National Park and ends at the forest's Molino Basin Campground. This segment is open to hikers, equestrians and mountain bikers.

Segment 14	**Santa Catalina Mountains**
	Details: (520)749-8700

This segment of the trail is 18.8-miles long and is located in the Santa Catalina Ranger District of the Coronado National Forest. The segment begins at the Molino Basin Campground and ends at the junction of the Mount Lemmon Trail and the Sutherland Trail. 15.5 miles of the trail is located in the Pusch Ridge Wilderness and is closed to mountain bikes.

Segment 15 Oracle Ridge 🚶 🐎 🚵
Details: (520)749-8700
Most of this 23.8-mile segment of the trail, which begins at the junction of the Sutherland and Mount Lemmon Trails and ends at the forest boundary near the American Flag Trailhead, is open to hikers, equestrians and mountain bikers. The first 1.5 miles of the segment is located in the Pusch Ridge Wilderness and is closed to bicycles. The entire segment is located in the Santa Catalina Ranger District of the Coronado National Forest.

Segment 16 Oracle 🚶 🐎 🚵
Details: (520)896-2425
This 8-mile long segment consists of 1 mile of trail across Arizona State Trust Land and 7 miles of trail within Oracle State Park. The segment begins at the boundary of the Santa Catalina Ranger District of the Coronado National Forest and ends at State Highway 77 near Oracle. The Oracle segment is open to hikers, equestrians and mountain bikers.

Juan Bautista de Anza National Historic Trail

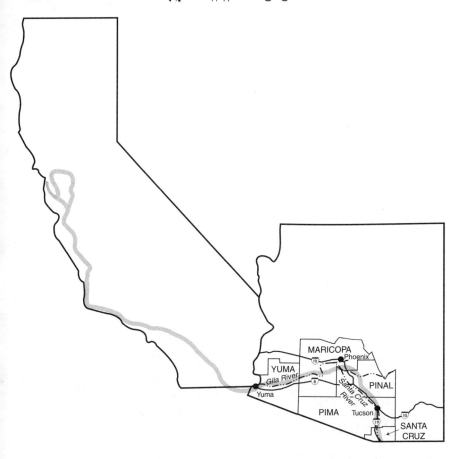

There are 11 National Historic Trails in the United States, and southern Arizona is home to an important segment of one of them—the Juan Bautista de Anza National Historic Trail. The trail is named for Spanish explorer and military officer Juan Bautista de Anza, and commemorates the 1,200-mile overland route he followed in 1775–76 while leading a group of colonists from Horcasitas, Sonora, Mexico on an expedition to establish a presidio and mission in the name of Spain at what is now San Francisco Bay. A map of the route taken by Anza and his entourage through Arizona and California appears above.

The southern Arizona counties that are home to sections of the Anza Trail (Santa Cruz, Pima, Pinal, Maricopa, and Yuma) are working with the Anza Trail Coalition of Arizona and the National Park Service to preserve, develop and interpret the Anza Trail. Although the Anza Trail project is still in its earliest stages, several sections of the trail in Pima County are open to public use. These sections include a 4.5-mile stretch between the National Park Service's Tumacacori National Historical Park and the State of Arizona's Tubac Presidio State Historic Park open to pedestrians and equestrians, and two segments totaling 4.5 miles that share the west bank of the Santa Cruz River Park in Tucson (Irvington Road to Ajo Way and Silverlake Road to Grant Road) that are open to hikers and bicyclists. Staging areas for the Santa Cruz River Park are shown on the Pima County River Parks map on page 34.

Several sections of the Anza Trail in the Green Valley area have recently been acquired by Pima County, and in May, 1997, Pima County voters approved $850,000 in bond funding that will be used to acquire and develop additional segments of the trail over the next nine years. In addition, the provision of an easement for a 14-mile segment of the Anza Trail in Santa Cruz County may be provided by Rio Rico Properties. For more information, call the Pima County Parks and Recreation Department at (520)740-2690.

Recommended reading:
- *Comprehensive Management and Use Plan, Juan Bautista De Anza National Historic Trail*, by U.S. Department of the Interior, National Park Service, Pacific West Field Area
- *Juan Bautista de Anza National Historic Trail*, by Don Garate

The Arizona State Trails Program

In 1972, the Arizona State Parks Board established the Arizona State Trails Program to preserve, develop, and promote nonmotorized recreational trail opportunities throughout the state, and placed the program under the management of Arizona State Parks. At the same time, the board created a committee, now known as the Arizona State Committee on Trails (ASCOT) to provide advice and assistance to the board and the agency on trails matters. ASCOT is composed of 25 members from land management agencies, trails groups, and the private sector, all of whom are appointed to ASCOT by the State Parks Board. ASCOT also maintains an advisory committee; any interested trails enthusiast can be a member. State Parks hired its first State Trails Coordinator in 1986, who, in addition to coordinating the State Trails Program, also serves as staff to ASCOT.

The State Trails Program works with ASCOT to develop the State Trails Plan, oversee the State Trails System, publish a State Trails Guide, support the development of long distance trails, research and document historic trails, assist efforts to secure access to trails on public lands, promote trail etiquette, provide technical assistance to land management agencies, support beneficial legislation, and stage a biannual State Trails

Conference. For additional information about the State Trails Program or ASCOT, call the State Trails Coordinator at (602)542-7116, or write c/o Arizona State Parks, 1300 W. Washington St., Phoenix, AZ 85007.

Recommended reading:
- *Arizona State Trails Guide*, by Arizona State Parks and ASCOT
- *Arizona State Trails Plan*, by Arizona State Parks and ASCOT

The Arizona Off-Highway Vehicle Program and Fund

The motorized counterpart to the Arizona State Trails Program is the **State Off-Highway Vehicle Program**, which was established by the State Legislature and Governor Mofford in 1989. The OHV Program, also located within the Arizona State Parks Department, works to develop and enhance OHV recreation opportunities around the state, and engages in educational activities that promote user safety and the responsible use of off-highway vehicles.

The Arizona State OHV Program is managed by the State OHV Program Coordinator, who also serves as staff to the seven-member State OHV Advisory Group (OHVAG), the members of which are appointed by the Arizona State Parks Board. The program coordinator and OHVAG jointly oversee the State OHV Recreation Fund, a gas-tax derived grant program that makes approximately $1.8 million available each year to government agencies at all levels to improve OHV recreation and access opportunities in Arizona. The gas taxes are paid by OHV users, which makes the OHV Recreation Fund a user-fee/user benefit program. For additional information about the State OHV Program, call the OHV Program Coordinator at (602)542-7115, or write c/o Arizona State Parks Department, 1300 W. Washington St., Phoenix, AZ 85007.

Recommended reading:
- *Arizona State OHV Recreation Plan*, by the Arizona State Parks Department

The Arizona Heritage Fund

In 1990, the voters of Arizona approved a grassroots initiative to establish the Arizona Heritage Fund, a grant program that receives $20 million in proceeds from the Arizona Lottery each year. Through the Arizona Game and Fish Department and Arizona State Parks Department, the Heritage Fund provides money for a variety of worthwhile projects, including natural resource conservation, environmental education, historic preservation, and the development of recreational trails.

The impact of the Heritage Fund has been profound. Heritage Fund dollars have been used to help restore the Mission San Xavier del Bac, establish the Sonoita Creek Natural Area, and develop more than 300 miles of trails and a myriad of trails facilities around the state, including the Arizona Trail. For more information about the Arizona Heritage Fund and how you can protect and support it, contact the Arizona Heritage Alliance at 110 W. Camelback Rd., Suite 201-F, Phoenix, AZ, 85013 (602)266-6586. Becoming a member of the Alliance, a citizen's group dedicated to the protection of Heritage Fund, will help ensure that this very worthwhile grant program continues to provide funding for Arizona trail projects in the years to come.

Pima County Trails and Open Space Program

The Pima County Trails and Open Space program began in 1989, when the Pima County Board of Supervisors adopted the **Eastern Pima County Trail System Master Plan**, a comprehensive inventory of the Tucson metro area's existing recreational trail resources. The program is located within the Pima County Parks and Recreation Department, which hired a full-time trails and open space coordinator to manage the effort in January, 1995.

The program's principal activities include working to protect and preserve the more than 1,000 miles of recreational trails in the Tucson metro area listed on the Eastern Pima County Trail System Master Plan, assuring access to the region's public lands jurisdictions (such as the Coronado National Forest and Saguaro National Park), trail and trailhead planning and development, natural resource park planning, volunteer coordination, assisting trails groups and other agencies, identifying key open space for protection and acquisition, and much more. The department maintains a 40-member Trails Advisory Committee composed of local trail users and agency representatives, and is a member of the Arizona State Committee on Trails (ASCOT). For additional information about the county's trails and open space program, or to inquire about volunteer opportunities, contact the county trails and open space coordinator at (520)740-2690, or write 1204 W. Silverlake Rd., Tucson, AZ 85713.

Recommended reading:
- *Eastern Pima County Trail System Master Plan*, by Pima County Parks and Recreation Department/Dames and Moore, 1989

National Trails Day

National Trails Day was established in 1993 by the American Hiking Society (AHS) and several private sector sponsors to promote the many benefits of recreational trails, as well as to encourage trails-related voluntarism, foster the development of partnerships between agencies, trail users and the outdoor industry, and to highlight the importance of natural resource protection.

National Trails Day occurs each year on the first Saturday in June, and is celebrated in a variety of ways. National Trails Day events in Pima County have included the dedication of trailhead facilities, trail maintenance and cleanup projects, group rides and hikes, and the recognition of trails volunteers. To take part in National Trails Day festivities, or for more information about staging an National Trails Day event of your own, contact Pima Trails Association at P.O. Box 41358, Tucson, Arizona, 85717, the American Hiking Society at P.O. Box 20160, Washington, D.C. 20041 (301)565-6704, or call the Pima County Parks and Recreation Department at (520)740-2690.

Doing Your Part: Volunteering for Trails

It's a sad fact of life. Lots of people use and enjoy trails, but few volunteer to help plan, manage, and maintain them. Unfortunately, in this age of shrinking government budgets, the need for trails volunteers has never been greater. The authors believe that every trail user should take the time to volunteer for trails, and with such a large variety of opportunities available, there's no excuse not to lend a hand. All of the land management agencies and organizations listed throughout the *Guide* can put volunteers to work. The following is a sampling of the kinds of opportunities that are available:

- Anza Trail Coalition
  Trail planning and development, newsletter, fundraising, education/interpretation

- Arizona Heritage Alliance
  Advocacy, education and outreach, newsletter, fundraising

- Arizona State Committee on Trails (ASCOT)/Arizona State Trails Program
  Advisory group participation, project, event, and conference assistance

- Arizona State Parks
  ASCOT Advisory Group, Site Stewards Program, Adopt-A-Trail, OHV Advisory Group

- Arizona Trail Association
  Advocacy, trail planning, trail construction and maintenance, volunteer coordination, event and project coordination, fundraising, education and interpretation, newsletter

- Bureau of Land Management
  Trail maintenance, citizen participation in planning efforts, project assistance

- Coronado National Forest
  Trail maintenance, visitor services, project assistance

- Empire Ranch Foundation
  Historic preservation activities, program development, project planning, fundraising

- Huachuca Hiking Club
  Advocacy, trail building and maintenance, event assistance, newsletter

- Pima Trails Association
  Advocacy, trail maintenance, newsletter, fundraising, event coordination, special projects

- Pima County Parks and Recreation Department
  Trail patrols, reserve park rangers, trail maintenance, Adopt-A-Trail, Pima County Trails Advisory Committee
- Pima County Mounted Sheriff's Posse
  Search and rescue assistance, trail maintenance, advocacy
- Saguaro National Park
  Foot, bike and horse-based trail patrols, trail maintenance, visitor services, interpretation
- Southern Arizona Hiking Club
  Trail maintenance, advocacy, newsletter, hike leaders
- Southern Arizona Mountain Bike Association
  Trail maintenance, dealer and rider outreach
- Student Conservation Association
  Trail maintenance and construction, interpretive and other resource assistance programs
- Southern Arizona Rescue Association
  Backcountry search and rescue assistance and support
- Thunder Mountain Trekkers
  Trails advocacy, trail maintenance and cleanup, newsletter, event assistance, fundraising
- Tucson Saddle Club
  Advocacy, trail and ranch maintenance (Adopt-A-Ranch), newsletter, event coordination

Directory of Trails Organizations

Trails Advocacy Groups

Anza Trail Coalition of Arizona
A nonprofit advocacy group working to protect and develop the Juan Bautista de Anza National Historic Trail in southern Arizona. Membership, newsletter, volunteer opportunities.
Maricopa Chapter:
  2741 E. Larkspur Dr.
  Phoenix, AZ 85032
Pima Chapter:
  P.O. Box 42612
  Tucson, AZ 85733
  (520)325-0909
Pinal Chapter:
  P.O. Box 1175
  Red Rock, AZ 85245
  (520)682-2510
Santa Cruz Chapter:
  P.O. Box 396
  Tumacacori, AZ 85640
  (520)398-2150
Yuma Chapter:
  240 Madison Avenue
  Yuma, AZ 85364
  (520)782-1841

Arizona Heritage Alliance
110 W. Camelback Rd., Suite 201-F
Phoenix, AZ 85013
(602)266-6586
A 375-member nonprofit citizens group working to protect and enhance the Arizona Heritage Fund. Membership, newsletter, volunteer opportunities.

Arizona Off-Highway Vehicle Association (AOHVA)
9430 E. Golf Links Rd., Suite 230
Tucson, AZ 85730-1337
(520)885-8842
A nonprofit advocacy group representing the interests of Off-Highway Vehicle enthusiasts. Membership, newsletter, volunteer opportunities.

Arizona State Committee on Trails (ASCOT)
c/o Arizona State Parks
1300 W. Washington St.
Phoenix, AZ 85007
(602)542-7116
A 25-member group that advises the State Parks Board on trails matters. Members are appointed by the State Parks Board. The ASCOT advisory committee is open to interested trails enthusiasts.

Arizona Trail Association (ATA)
P.O. Box 36736
Phoenix, AZ 85067
(602)252-4794
An all-volunteer nonprofit group working to establish the 800-mile, cross-state Arizona Trail by the Year 2000. Membership, newsletter, volunteer opportunities.

Awareness to Access, Inc.
3881 W. Sunny Shadows Pl.
Tucson, AZ 85741
(520)744-4039
A nonprofit, all-volunteer advocacy organization working to generate wilderness access for physically-challenged users through greater awareness.

Off-Highway Vehicle Advisory Group (OHVAG)
c/o Arizona State Parks
1300 W. Washington St.
Phoenix, AZ 85007
(602)542-7115
A seven-member group that advises the State Parks Board on OHV matters. Members are appointed by the State Parks Board.

Oracle Trails Coalition
P.O. Box 700
Oracle, AZ 85623
(520)896-2425
A nonprofit shared-use trails advocacy group. Membership, volunteer opportunities.

Pima Trails Association
P.O. Box 41358
Tucson, AZ 85717
(520)577-7919
A nonprofit shared-use trails advocacy group working to protect, preserve and

develop recreational trails in Pima County. Membership, newsletter, volunteer opportunities.

Santa Cruz Valley Coalition for Open Space, Trails and Parks
P.O. Box 266
Green Valley, AZ 85622
(520)625-6365
An informal advocacy group working to protect the historic, recreational and cultural resources of the Santa Cruz Valley area. Membership, volunteer opportunities.

Trails Clubs

Arizona State Association of Four-Wheel Drive Clubs
P.O. Box 30295
Mesa, AZ 85275
(602)832-8132
A nonprofit association of 4x4 clubs working to promote the responsible use of four-wheel drive vehicles and the development and maintenance of 4x4 recreational opportunities. Membership, newsletter, volunteer opportunities.

Arizona State Horsemen's Association
P.O. Box 31758
Phoenix, AZ 85006
(602)258-2708
A federation of riding groups affiliated with the American Horse Council that stages rides and engages in advocacy. Membership, newsletter, volunteer opportunities.

Casa Grande 4 Wheelers, Inc.
P.O. Box 12891
Casa Grande, AZ 85230
(520)836-3016
A 25-family nonprofit 4x4 club that stages day and overnight outings and engages in trails advocacy. Membership, newsletter, volunteer opportunities.

Cochise County Range Riders
P.O. Box 532
Fort Huachuca, AZ 85613
(520)458-6148
A 35-member nonprofit, family-oriented 4x4 club that offers day and weekend trips and engages in trails advocacy. Membership, newsletter, volunteer opportunities.

County Line Riders Association of Catalina
13980 N. Dust Devil Dr.
Tucson, AZ 85737
(520)825-7609
A 150-member nonprofit equestrian club that leads rides, works with land agencies and engages in advocacy. Membership, volunteer opportunities.

Greater Arizona Bicycling Association
A 900-member nonprofit cycling club that leads road and mountain bike rides and stages events. Membership, newsletter, events, volunteer opportunities.
Tucson Chapter
P.O. Box 43273
Tucson, AZ 85733
(520)721-2808
Cochise Chapter
P.O. Box 3618
Sierra Vista, AZ 85636
(520)378-6890

Green Valley Recreation Hiking Club
P.O. Box 1074
Green Valley, AZ 85622
(520)625-3440
A 350-member hiking club organized by the Green Valley Recreation Association that leads hikes year-round. Club is open only to members of the association.

Huachuca Hiking Club
P.O. Box 3555
Sierra Vista, AZ 85636
(520)459-8959
A 40-member hiking club that leads hikes, conducts trail construction and maintenance projects, and engages in advocacy. Membership, newsletter, volunteer opportunities.

Nomads Off-Highway Vehicle Club
4862 San Molino St.
Sierra Vista, AZ 85635
(520)378-0553
A 25-year-old, 100-member nonprofit off-road motorcycle and ATV club that operates its own track and works with land management agencies. Membership, newsletter, volunteer opportunities.

Pima County Mounted Sheriff's Posse
8987-309 E. Tanque Verde Rd., Box 232
Tucson, AZ 85749
(520)298-7716
A nonprofit, all-volunteer group of equestrians that assists the Pima County Sheriff's Department with search and rescue and community activities, including the Rodeo Parade. Membership, volunteer opportunities.

Ridge Running Rovers/Land Rover Owners Group
A 38-member nonprofit OHV Club that leads monthly trips, teaches off-road driving classes, engages in advocacy and works with land agencies. Membership, newsletter, volunteer opportunities.

Santa Cruz Valley Horsemen's Association
P.O. Box 266
Green Valley, AZ 85622
(520)625-6365
A 55-member recreational riding club that also engages in trails advocacy in the Green Valley area. Membership, newsletter, volunteer opportunities.

Senior Trekkers Club
c/o 250 N. Maguire Ave.
Tucson, AZ 85710
(520)296-7795
A 100-member hiking and walking club for people over 50. Events include weekly walks in Sabino Canyon.

Southern Arizona Hiking Club
P.O. Box 32257
Tucson, AZ 85751
(520)751-4513
An 1800-member recreational hiking club established in 1958. Offers 50-60 hikes each month. Membership, newsletter, volunteer opportunities.

Southern Arizona Mountain Bike Association (SAMBA)
P.O. Box 85456
Tucson, AZ 85754-5456
(520)882-0965
A 100-member mountain biking club established in 1991. Offers four club rides each month on alternating Saturdays and Sundays, as well as riding skills training and maintenance classes. Membership, newsletter, volunteer opportunities.

Southern Arizona Roadrunners
4625 E. Broadway Blvd., #112
Tucson, AZ 85711
(520)326-9383
A 1000-member running club that stages ten competitive races each year, as well as 11 casual monthly run/walks for all ages and fitness levels. Membership, newsletter, volunteer opportunities.

Tucson Mountains Riders
6394 N. Yuma Mine Rd.
Tucson, AZ 85743
(520)579-1397
A 60-member equestrian club that stages recreational rides and events and engages in trails advocacy. Membership, newsletter, volunteer opportunities.

Thunder Mountain Trekkers
3288 S. Sky Hawk Dr.
Sierra Vista, AZ 85635
(520)378-1763
A 55-member nonprofit club that stages ten walking and cycling events each year based on the volkssport concept. Membership, newsletter, volunteer opportunities.

Tucson Orienteering Club
P.O. Box 13012
Tucson, AZ 85732
(520)628-8985
An 80-member orienteering club affiliated with the U.S. Orienteering Federation. Membership, newsletter, volunteer opportunities.

Tucson Rough Riders
P.O. Box 78726
Tucson, AZ 85703
(520)795-8102
A four-wheel-drive enthusiasts club that stages group drives and events, and also engages in advocacy and volunteer projects. Membership, newsletter, volunteer opportunities.

Tucson Saddle Club
P.O. Box 30433
Tucson, AZ 85751
(520)298-7716
A 150-member nonprofit riding club that engages in trails and equestrian advocacy. Membership, newsletter, volunteer opportunities.

Tucson Volkssport Klub
270 S. Candlestick Dr.
Tucson, AZ 85748
(520)298-4340
A noncompetitive recreational walking and biking club that offers a variety of events based on the volkssport concept. Membership, newsletter, volunteer opportunities.

University of Arizona Ramblers Hiking Club
UA Student Union Activities Center
University of Arizona
Tucson, AZ 85721
(520)621-8046
An informal hiking club founded at the UA in the 1950s. Club averages ten hikes and backpacking trips each month. Most members are students or former students, but anyone can participate. Membership, volunteer opportunities.

Conservation Groups with Trails Interests

Arizona Nature Conservancy, The
300 E. University Blvd.
Tucson, AZ 85705
(520)622-3861
A national conservation organization promoting the preservation of natural areas and wildlife and through private nature preserve ownership and trusts. Membership, newsletter, volunteer opportunities.

Audubon Society
The Society promotes conservation and environmental education with community-based programs for children and adults. Membership, newsletter, volunteer opportunities.
Huachuca Chapter
P.O. Box 63
Sierra Vista, AZ 85636
(520)432-4634
Tucson Chapter
300 E. University Blvd., Suite 120
Tucson, AZ 85705
(520)629-0510
Yuma Chapter
P.O. Box 6395
Yuma, AZ 85366
(520)782-3552

Empire Ranch Foundation
12661 E. Broadway Blvd.
Tucson, AZ 85748
(520)722-4289
A nonprofit group working with the U.S. Bureau of Land Management to protect and enhance the historic, recreational and natural resources of the Empire-Cienega Resource Conservation Area (RCA). Membership, newsletter, volunteer opportunities.

Friends of Madera Canyon
P.O. Box 1203
Green Valley, AZ 85622
(520)625-5218
A nonprofit group working with the U.S. Forest Service to protect and enhance Madera Canyon. Membership, newsletter, volunteer opportunities.

Friends of Sabino Canyon
P.O. Box 2022
Tucson, AZ 85702
(520)749-8700
A nonprofit group working with the U.S. Forest Service to protect and enhance Sabino Canyon. Membership, newsletter, volunteer opportunities.

Friends of Saguaro National Park
P.O. Box 18998
Tucson, AZ
(520)298-3258
A nonprofit group working with the National Park Service to protect and enhance Saguaro National Park. Membership, newsletter, volunteer opportunities.

Friends of the San Pedro River
1763 Paseo San Luis
Sierra Vista, AZ 85622
(520)459-2555
A nonprofit group working with the U.S. Bureau of Land Management to protect and enhance the San Pedro Riparian National Conservation Area. Membership, newsletter, volunteer opportunities.

Rincon Institute
7650 E. Broadway Blvd.
Tucson, AZ 85710
(520)290-0828
Fax: (520)290-0969
A nonprofit conservation group working to protect the sensitive ecosystems of Saguaro National Park and the adjacent Rincon Valley. Also involved in trails planning in the Rincon Valley. Membership, newsletter, volunteer opportunities.

Sierra Club
A national nonprofit group founded in 1892 by John Muir to promote the study, protection and responsible use of the Earth's ecosystems and resources. Membership, newsletter, volunteer opportunities.
Tucson (Rincon Chapter)
738 N. 5th Ave., #214, Tucson, AZ 85705
(520)620-6401

National Trails Groups

American Hiking Society (AHS)
P.O. Box 20160
Washington, D.C. 20041
(301) 565-6704
Fax: (301)565-6714
A nonprofit trails advocacy group dedicated to the promotion of hiking and the protection, maintenance and development of foot trails in America. Coordinates National Trails Day. Membership, newsletter.

American Horse Council (AHC)
1700 K Street NW, Suite 300
Washington, D.C. 20006
(202)296-4031
Fax: (202)296-1970
A 2,200-member equestrian advocacy group that lobbies Congress to promote the interests of horse owners and the horse industry. Membership, newsletter.

American Trails
P.O. Box 11046
Prescott, AZ 86304
(520)632-1140
Fax: (520)632-1147
e-mail: AmTrails@lankaster.com
A nonprofit trails advocacy group dedicated to the promotion, creation and protection of trail systems for all Americans. An advocate of shared-use trails. Stages the National Trails Symposium every two years. Membership, newsletter, volunteer opportunities.

International Mountain Bicycling Association (IMBA)
P.O. Box 7578
Boulder, CO 80306
(303)545-901
Fax: (303)545-9026
A 7000-member trail access advocacy group working to promote mountain bicycling that is socially and environmentally responsible. Membership, newsletter, volunteer opportunities.

National Off-Highway Vehicle Conservation Council (NOHVCC)
1020 Superior Ave.
Sheboygan, WI 53081
1-800-348-6487
Fax: (920) 458-3446
A nonprofit advocacy group working to promote the development of OHV recreation opportunities and the safe, environmentally sound use of Off-Highway Vehicles.

Rails-to-Trails Conservancy (RTC)
1100 17th Street NW (10th Floor)
Washington, D.C. 20036
(202)331-9696
Fax: (202)331-9680
A nonprofit advocacy group leading the effort to convert abandoned railroad corridors into public "Rail Trails" nationwide. Membership, newsletter, volunteer opportunities.

Student Conservation Association, Inc. (SCA)
P.O. Box 550
Charleston, NH 03603-0550
(603)543-1700
Fax: (603)543-1828
A nonprofit group that operates three volunteer programs: the Resource Assistant Program for adults, a High School Program, and a Conservation Care Development Program. SCA places approximately 2,000 persons in volunteer conservation projects each year. Write for a catalog.

Trails Publications

The trails-related publications listed in this section of the *Guide* are all in print and should be readily available through outdoors stores, book vendors, public agencies and libraries around Tucson and southern Arizona. If you have trouble locating any of these books or periodicals, ask your bookseller for assistance or contact the publisher directly.

Publications of General Interest:

Adventuring in Arizona, John Annerino, Sierra Club Books, San Francisco, CA, 1996

Arizona's Natural Environment, Charles H. Lowe, University of Arizona Press, Tucson, AZ, 1985

Arizona State Trails Guide, Arizona State Committee on Trails, Arizona State Parks, Phoenix, AZ, 1995

Arizona Traveler's Handbook (5th Edition), Bill Weir and Robert Blake, Moon Publications, Inc., Chico, CA, 1995

BLM Wilderness Area Maps and Information, USDI Bureau of Land Management, Phoenix, AZ

Complete Walker III, The, Colin Fletcher, Alfred A. Knopf, Inc., NY, 1986

Comprehensive Management and Use Plan and Final Environmental Impact Statement, Juan Bautista de Anza National Historic Trail, U.S. Department of the Interior, National Park Service, Pacific West Field Area, San Francisco, CA, 1996

Deserts, James A. McMahon, The Audubon Society Nature Guides, Alfred A. Knopf, Inc., New York, NY, 1985

Discovering Tucson: A Guide to the Old Pueblo and Beyond, Carolyn Grossman and Suzanne Myal, Fiesta Publishing, Tucson, AZ 1996

Historical Atlas of Arizona, Henry P. Walker and Don Bufkin, University of Oklahoma Press, Norman, OK, 1986

Juan Bautista de Anza National Historic Trail, Don Garate, Southwest Parks and Monuments Association, Tucson, AZ, 1994

Mountains Next Door, The, Janice Bowers, University of Arizona Press, Tucson, AZ, 1991

Paradise Found: The Settlement of the Santa Catalina Mountains, Kathy Alexander, Skunkworks Productions, Mt. Lemmon, AZ, 1991

Roadside Geology of Arizona, Halka Chronic, Mountain Press Publishing Co., Missoula, MO, 1983

Sabino Canyon: Life of a Southwestern Oasis, D. Lazaroff, University of Arizona Press, Tucson, AZ, 1993

Scenic Tucson, Bob Kerry, Backcountry Books of Arizona, Tucson, AZ 1994

Southern Arizona Nature Almanac, Roseann Beggy Hanson and Jonathan Hanson, Pruett Publishing Company, Boulder, CO, 1996

Trails of Southeastern Arizona—Arizona State Trails Guide (3rd Edition), Arizona State Parks and the Arizona State Committee on Trails (ASCOT) Phoenix, AZ, 1994 (602)542-7116

Trails of Southwestern Arizona—Arizona State Trails Guide (3rd Edition), Arizona State Parks and the Arizona State Committee on Trails (ASCOT) Phoenix, AZ, 1994 (602)542-7116

Western Forests, Stephen Whitney, The Audubon Society Nature Guides, Alfred A. Knopf, inc., New York, NY, 1985

Outdoor Preparedness and First Aid Books

Be Expert with Map and Compass, Bjorn Hjellstrom, Macmillan Co., New York, NY, 1994

Desert Survival Handbook, Charles A. Lehman, Primer Publishers, Phoenix, AZ, 1993

Far From Help!: Backcountry Medical Care, Peter Steele, published by Cloudcap, Seattle, WA, 1991

Land Navigation Handbook: The Sierra Club Guide to Map and Compass, W. S. Kals, Sierra Club Books, San Francisco, CA, 1983

Leave No Trace Outdoor Skills and Ethics: Desert and Canyon Country, National Outdoor Leadership School, Lander, WY, 1994

Medicine for the Backcountry, Buck Tilton, M. S. and Frank Hubbel, D.O., ICS Books, Inc., Merrilville, IN, 1994

Mountaineering First Aid: A Guide to Accident Response and First Aid Care, Martha J. Lentza, Ph.D., R.N., et al, The Mountaineers, Seattle, WA, 1990

Mountaineering: The Freedom of the Hills, The Mountaineers, Seattle, WA, 1996

Pocket Doctor, The: Your Guide to Good Health While Traveling, Stephen Bezruchka, M.D., The Mountaineers, Seattle, WA, 1988

Ten Essentials for Travel in the Outdoors, The, The Mountaineers, Seattle, WA, 1993

Wilderness Basics: The Complete Handbook for Hikers and Backpackers, The San Diego Chapter of the Sierra Club, published by The Mountaineers, Seattle, WA, 1993

Hiking Guides

Arizona Day Hikes, Dave Ganci, Sierra Club Books, San Francisco, CA, 1995

Arizona's Mountains, Bob and Dotty Martin, Cordillera Press, Evergreen, CO, 1991

Arizona Trails: 100 Hikes in Canyon and Sierra, David Mazel, Wilderness Press, Berkeley, CA, 1996. Distributed by Treasure Chest Publications (800) 969-9558.

Desert Hiking, Dave Ganci, Wilderness Press, Berkeley Press, Berkeley, CA, 1983

Exploring Arizona's Wild Areas: A Guide for Hikers, Backpackers, Climbers, X-C Skiers, and Paddlers, Scott S. Warren, The Mountaineers, Seattle, WA, 1986

Hiker's Guide to Arizona, The, Stewart Aitchison and Bruce Grubbs, Falcon Press Publishing Co., Inc., Helena, MT, 1992

Hiker's Guide to the Huachuca Mountains, Leonard Taylor, Banner Printing, Sierra Vista, AZ, 1991

Hiker's Guide to the Santa Rita Mountains, Betty Leavengood and Mike Liebert, Pruett Publishing Co., Boulder, CO, 1994

Hiking Arizona's Cactus Country, Erik Molvar, Falcon Press, Helena, MT, 1995

Hiking Southern Arizona, Don R. Kiefer, Golden West Publishers, Phoenix, AZ, 1995

Hiking Trails and Wilderness Routes of the Chiricahua Mountains, Cachor Taylor, Rainbow Expeditions, Tucson, AZ, 1977

100 Hikes in Arizona, Scott Warren, The Mountaineers, Seattle, WA, 1994

Outdoors in Arizona: A Guide to Hiking and Backpacking, John Annerino, Arizona Highways, Phoenix, AZ, 1996

Southern Arizona Trails, David Mazel and Robert Blake, Wilderness Press, Berkeley, CA, 1997

Trail Guide to the Santa Catalina Mountains, Eber Glendening and Pete Cowgill, Rainbow Expeditions, Tucson, AZ, 1987

Tucson Hiking Guide, Betty Leavengood, Pruett Publishing Co., Boulder, CO, 1997 (2nd edition)

Equestrian and Trail Stock Publications

Horse Trails in Arizona, Jan Hancock, Golden West Publishers, Inc., Phoenix, AZ, 1994

Goat Tracks (quarterly periodical), published by Ellen McMaster, Washougal, WA, 8671

Pack Goat, The, John Mionczynski, Pruett Publishing, Boulder, CO 1992

Treading Lightly with Pack Animals: A Guide to Low Impact Travel in the Backcountry, Dan Aadland, Mountain Press Publishing Co., Missoula, MT, 1993

Mountain Biking Publications

Bike Tours in Southern Arizona, Mort Solot and Philip Varney, Breakaway Press, Tucson, AZ, 1991

Fat Tire Tales and Trails: Mountain Bike Fun in Arizona, Cosmic Ray, self-published, Flagstaff, AZ, 1995

Mountain Biking Arizona, Sarah Bennett, Menasha Press, Birmingham, AL, 1995. Distributed by Falcon Press, Helena, MT

Mountain Biking the Old Pueblo, Michael Jimmerson and Jim Porter, Post Litho Printing, Tucson, AZ, 1992

Mountain Bike Rides in the Tucson Area, Chris Guibert and Robert Reed, Arizona Offroad Adventures, Tucson, AZ, 1997

Off-Highway Vehicle Publications

Arizona Off-Road Vehicle Recreation Guide, Arizona State Parks, Phoenix, AZ, 1997

Arizona State OHV Plan, Arizona State Parks Board/Arizona State University Department of Recreation Management and Tourism, Tempe, AZ, 1993

Backroads and Beyond: By Truck and Foot in Southern Arizona, Pete Cowgill, Broken Arrow Press, Tucson, AZ 1997

Four Wheel Drive Trails of Arizona, The, Scott Deuty, 4x4 Travel, Gilbert, AZ 1996

Travel Arizona: The Back Roads, James E. Cook et al, Arizona Highways, Phoenix, AZ 1996

Barrier Free Publications

Access Arizona: An Atlas and Travel Guide for Disabled and Mature Travelers to Major Outdoor Recreation Areas, Arizona State Parks, Phoenix, AZ, 1991

Recreation Guide to Barrier-Free Facilities, Southwestern National Forests, USDA Forest Service, Southwestern Regional Office, Albuquerque, NM, 1993

Universal Access to Outdoor Recreation: A Design Guide, David Driskell, PLAE, Inc., Berkeley, CA 1993

Trails Advocacy, Planning, Construction and Maintenance Publications

Arizona State Trails Plan, Arizona State Parks and Arizona State Committee on Trails, Phoenix, AZ, 1994

Arizona Trail Management Guide, Arizona State Parks, Phoenix, AZ, 1994

Eastern Pima County Trail System Master Plan, Pima County Parks and Recreation Department/Dames and Moore, Tucson, AZ, 1989, (Revised 1996)

Lightly on the Land: The SCA Trail Building and Maintenance Manual, Robert C. Birkby, published by The Mountaineers, Seattle, WA, 1996

Pima County River Parks Master Plan, Pima County Department of Transportation and Flood Control District/Planners Ink, Tucson, AZ, 1996

Public Trail Access: A Guide to the Protection of Arizona's Trails, Arizona State Committee on Trails (ASCOT), Arizona State Parks, Phoenix, AZ. 1992

Introduction to Basic Trail Maintenance, Kurt Loheit and Frank Padilla, Jr., International Mountain Bicycling Association, Boulder, CO, 1995

Trail Construction and Maintenance Notebook, USDA Forest Service, Missoula, MT, 1996

Maps and Map Sources

Noteworthy maps for the Southern Arizona area include:

Arizona Atlas and Gazetteer, DeLorme Mapping, Freeport, ME, 1993. A book of topo maps that includes back roads and public lands information.

Arizona Road and Recreation Atlas, Benchmark Maps, Berkeley CA, 1996. Landscape and public lands maps of the entire state.

Arizona State Trails Guide, Arizona State Committee on Trails, Arizona State Parks, Phoenix, AZ, 1995. A comprehensive listing of all trails in the state trail system; includes route maps. Guide is divided into five volumes; Southeast and Southwest volumes cover southern Arizona.

Mountain Bike Rides of the Tucson Area, AZ Off-Road Adventures (Guibert/Reed), 1997. A comprehensive guide to riding opportunities in Tucson area, available at most bike shops and the sources listed below.

Saguaro National Park Trails Map, Trails Illustrated, Evergreen, CO, 1996. An outstanding topo map of both districts of the park, as well as part of Tucson Mountain Park.

Southern Arizona Hiking Club Maps. A well-developed series of topographic trail maps that cover the Santa Catalina, Santa Rita, Rincon, and Chiricahua Mountain areas; includes trail mileages. Available at outdoors stores and map vendors in the Tucson area.

USGS Topographical Maps. Available from the vendors listed below, these maps are the standard trail-user's tools. Maps are available in 7.5- and 15-minute quad sheets, but 15 minute quads are being phased out.

Benson
Southwest Map Center
730 W. 4th St. (520)586-2820

Sierra Vista
Livingston Books/Bookman's
108 W. Fry Blvd. (520)458-9702

Tucson
Arizona Geological Survey
416 W. Congress St., Suite 100
(520)770-3500

Popular Outdoor Outfitters
2820 N. Campbell Ave. (520)326-2520
6314 N. Oracle Rd. (520)575-1044
6315 N. Broadway Blvd. (520)290-1644

Summit Hut
5045 E. Speedway Blvd. (520)325-1554

Tucson Map and Flag
3239 N. First Ave. (520)887-4234

Yuma
Nicholas Engineering
1851 W. 24th St. (520)344-8374

Popular Outdoor Outfitters
1111 S. 4th Ave. (520)783-8509

Sprague Sports and RV
345 W. 32nd St. (520)726-0022

Arizona Public Lands Information Center
222 N. Central Ave., Phoenix, AZ 85004-2203
(602)417-9300 FAX: (602)417-9556
E-mail: azplic@az.blm.gov
One of the best sources for maps and trails information in the state is the new Arizona Public Lands Information Center, which was established through a partnership between the U.S. Bureau of Land Management and the Southwest Natural and Cultural Heritage Association. The center, located at the BLM State Office in downtown Phoenix, can provide general information about all of Arizona's National Parks, National Forests, BLM and U.S. Fish and Wildlife Lands, and State Parks, State Trust Lands, and State Game and Fish Wildlife areas. The center also offers a comprehensive selection of maps, books, and guidebooks, including books for trail users of all kinds. Licenses and permits such as the Golden Eagle, Golden Age, and State Park Annual Permits are available at the center as well.

Notes

Notes

Membership Application

(please type or print)

YES, I CAN VOLUNTEER _____

Date: _____

Pima Trails Association

Name: _____

Address: _____

City: _____ State: _____ ZIP: _____

Home # _____ Work # _____

Membership in other groups: _____

How do you use the trails? (hike, bike, horse, etc.) _____

_____

Skills/occupation you can contribute to PTA: _____

_____

Yearly Membership Fee:
$10 student (full-time student)
$15 individual
$25 family (includes 2 adults and any children under 21)
$30 organization/business
The membership year is January 1 thru December 31.
No memberships are prorated.

Contributions are always welcome and are tax-deductible.
Make checks payable to: Pima Trails Association
Mail all checks to:
PTA Membership
Post Office Box 41358
Tucson, Arizona 85717
Phone: (520) 577-7919

PTA Statement of Purpose

Pima Trails Association is a nonprofit, volunteer trails advocacy organization composed of hikers, equestrians and mountain bikers working together to protect and preserve trails in Pima County.

PTA Goals

1. Establish an integrated multi-use public trails system.
2. Assure permanent access to trails on public lands.
3. Promote cooperation with land owners and developers to preserve access to traditional-use trails on private lands.
4. Foster cooperation and communication among all trail user groups.
5. Communicate and cooperate with government agencies on trail matters.
6. Keep the community informed about trail issues and opportunities.
7. Facilitate the safe and harmonious multi-use of trails through trail education, community programs and fundraising activities.
8. Encourage the development of new recreational and historic trails.
9. Expand the effectiveness and influence of Pima Trails Association.